The Princeton Review®

TOEFL ®

Reading and Writing Workout

WITHDRAWN

By the Staff of The Princeton Review

PrincetonReview.com

PENGUIN RANDOM HOUSE

The Princeton Review
24 Prime Parkway, Suite 201
Natick, MA 01760
E-mail: editorialsupport@review.com

Published in the United States by Random House LLC, New York, and simultaneously in Canada by Random House of Canada Limited, Toronto.

A Penguin Random House Company.

ISBN: 978-0-8041-2594-9
ISSN: 2374-5428

The Princeton Review is not affiliated with Princeton University.

Editor: Calvin S. Cato
Production Editor: Emily Epstein White
Production Artist: Deborah A. Silvestrini

Printed in the United States of America on partially recycled paper.

10 9 8 7 6 5 4 3 2 1

Editorial

Rob Franek, Senior VP, Publisher
Casey Cornelius, VP Content Development
Mary Beth Garrick, Director of Production
Selena Coppock, Managing Editor
Calvin Cato, Editor
Colleen Day, Editor
Aaron Riccio, Editor
Meave Shelton, Editor
Orion McBean, Editorial Assistant

Random House Publishing Team

Tom Russell, Publisher
Alison Stoltzfus, Publishing Manager
Melinda Ackell, Associate Managing Editor
Ellen Reed, Production Manager
Kristin Lindner, Production Supervisor
Andrea Lau, Designer

Acknowledgments

The Princeton Review would like to thank Chad Chasteen, Orion McBean, Emily Epstein White, and Deborah Silvestrini for their hard work in the creation of this title. The Princeton Review would also like to thank Vanessa Coggshall for her work in the creation of the vocabulary drills.

Contents

...So Much More Online!

Register Your Book Now!

- Go to PrincetonReview.com and locate the "Register Books" entry form at the bottom right side of the website.

- Enter your book's ISBN in this space: 9780804125949. Please keep in mind to remove spaces and dashes from the number.

- Next you will see a SignUp/Sign In page where you will type in your E-mail address (username) and choose a password.

- Now you're good to go! You can access the audio files for *TOEFL Reading and Writing Workout* directly from PrincetonReview.com.

PrincetonReview.com

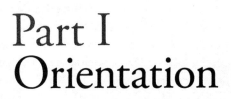

Part I
Orientation

WELCOME

Welcome to The Princeton Review's Reading and Writing Workout for the Test of English as a Foreign Language (TOEFL). In this book you'll find strategies and practice for two of the most important sections of the TOEFL.

This book is divided into three main parts.

- Part II of this book focuses on Vocabulary. In this section we review and quiz you on about 250 of the most commonly tested English words on the TOEFL.
- Part III focuses on Reading. In this section we review strategies and have practice Reading Drills.
- Part IV focuses on the Writing section. In this section we will review strategies and sample essays, and we will have some prompts for you to practice writing yoru own essays.

WHAT IS THE TOEFL?

The TOEFL is a test that assesses your proficiency in the type of English used in an academic environment. The test is administered on the Internet.

The exam takes about four hours to complete and integrates four essential skills—reading, listening, writing, and speaking. This means that any given question or task may require you to use one or more of these skills. For example, before attempting a writing task on the TOEFL, you may first have to read a passage and listen to a lecture on the topic.

Fortunately, the TOEFL is not as daunting as it may seem because it tests each of the four skills in a fairly specific ways. To become more comfortable with the type of writing, speaking, reading, and listening skills that are required to get a good score on the exam, pick up a copy of *Cracking the TOEFL iBT*, which offers a thorough review of the entire test.

STOP!

If it is difficult to understand the material on this page, it's best that you continue your study of basic English before taking the TOEFL. This book is intended to help students who already have knowledge of basic English, and our recommendation is that you should feel very comfortable with the language before you attempt to take the TOEFL.

THE STRUCTURE OF THE TEST

The TOEFL is broken down into four distinct sections, one for each of the skills previously listed. However, each section may require you to use more than one of these four skills. The structure of the test is as follows:

- One **Reading** section, consisting of three to four passages that are roughly 700 words each. Each passage will be followed by 12 to 14 multiple-choice questions about the content of the passage. Most of these questions will be worth one point each, though a few questions, located toward the end of the sections, may be worth more. Depending on the number of questions you see, you will have 60 to 80 minutes to complete the entire section.
- One **Listening** section, consisting of six to nine audio selections, each of which are three to five minutes long. The selections will consist of either academic lectures or casual conversations. After each selection, there will be five to six multiple-choice questions about the content of the lecture or conversation. You will have 60 to 90 minutes to complete the entire selection.
- One **Speaking** section, consisting of six speaking tasks. Most speaking tasks will also require some listening and some reading. Each task will require you to speak for 45 to 60 seconds, depending on the task, and you will have 20 minutes to complete the entire section.
- One **Writing** section, consisting of two writing assignments. The Writing section, like the Speaking section, also requires listening and some reading. You will have 50 minutes to complete the entire section.

HOW THE TEST IS SCORED

After finishing the TOEFL iBT, you will receive a score of from 0 to 30 for each of the four sections. You will also receive a total score on a scale of 0 to 120. Each score corresponds to a percentile ranking. This number shows how your score compares with the scores of other test takers. For example, a total score of 100 would put you in the 82nd percentile, meaning that you scored higher than 82 of 100 test takers, whereas a score of 68 would put you in the 25th percentile. The average TOEFL score is around 81.

Notice that the 0 to 30 scores are scaled scores, meaning that the 0 to 30 number doesn't represent how many questions you answered correctly or how many points your essay was awarded. For example, the Reading and Listening sections each contain roughly 40 questions. You will get a point for each correct answer (some Reading section questions will be worth two points) and there is no penalty for an incorrect answer. At the end of the section, your *raw* score, which represents how many points you've earned, is tallied and converted to a number on the 0 to 30 scale.

The Writing and Speaking sections are scored somewhat differently. Each writing sample receives a score of between 0 and 5. These raw scores are then converted to the 0 to 30 scale. Similarly, each speaking task receives a score from 0 to 4. The scores from all six speaking tasks are averaged and converted to the 0 to 30 scale.

HOW ARE THE SCORES USED?

Colleges and universities will look at your TOEFL score when considering your application. Of course, your TOEFL score is not the only factor that affects your chance of admission. Colleges and universities also look at your academic performance, letters of recommendation, application essays, and scores on other standardized tests. Although a high TOEFL score will not guarantee admission to a particular program, a low test score could jeopardize your chances.

Some schools and programs may require students with TOEFL scores below a certain cutoff score to take supplemental English classes. Others may accept only those applicants who score above a particular cutoff score. Make sure you check with the programs to which you are applying for specific information.

THE COMPUTER-BASED FORMAT USED FOR INTERNET-BASED TESTING (iBT)

The TOEFL is a computer-based test that is delivered to testing centers via the Internet; therefore, the TOEFL can be offered at locations throughout the world. The test is administered by Educational Testing Service (ETS), the same testing organization that administers the GRE, SAT, and other standardized tests. According to ETS, Internet-based testing (iBT) is an easier and fairer way to capture speech and to score responses. It also makes it possible for ETS to greatly expand access to test centers.

The iBT format will be new to the untrained eye and may be intimidating, especially if you have never taken a test on a computer. A brief tutorial is offered at the beginning of the TOEFL, in order to allow test takers time to familiarize themselves with the format. However, you should consider first taking a practice test so you're not surprised by the Internet format on test day because the iBT presents some challenges. For example, when working on a reading passage, you will see something similar to the following:

More Available

The Exoskeleton of the Arthropod

There are more arthropods alive on Earth than there are members of any other phylum of animals. Given that not only insects and spiders but also shrimp, crabs, centipedes, and their numerous relatives are arthropods, this fact should not occasion surprise. For all their diversity, arthropods of any type share two defining characteristics: jointed legs (from which the phylum takes its name) and an exoskeleton (the recognizable hard outer shell).

Though the shell itself is made of dead tissue like that of human hair and fingernails, it is dotted with sensory cells. These give the arthropod information about its surroundings, much as the nerve endings in human skin do. Also like human skin, the shell protects fragile internal organs from potentially hazardous contact with the environment. It seals in precious moisture that would otherwise evaporate but permits the exchange of gases.

Its primary component is chitin, a natural polymer that contains calcium and is very similar in structure to the cellulose in wood. Chitin and proteins are secreted in the epidermis, the living tissue just below the shell, after which they bond to form a thin sheet. Each new sheet is produced so that its chitin fibers are not parallel with those directly above, which increases their combined strength.

The result is the endocuticle, a mesh of molecules that forms the lowest layer of the shell. The endocuticle is not quite tough enough for daily wear and tear. Over time, however, its molecules continue to lock together. As the endocuticle is pushed upward by the formation of new sheets by

More Available

the epidermis, it becomes the middle shell layer called the exocuticle. With its molecules bonded so tightly, the exocuticle is very durable. There are points on the body where it does not form, since flexibility is needed around joints. This arrangement allows supple movement but provides armor-like protection.

Though strong, the chitin and protein exocuticle itself would provide a poor barrier against moisture loss. Therefore, it must be coated with lipids, which are also secreted by the epidermis. These lipids, mostly fatty acids and waxes, form the third, outermost layer of the shell. They spread over the cuticles to form a waterproof seal even in dry weather. This lipid layer gives many arthropods their distinctive luster.

Combined, the endocuticle, exocuticle, and lipid coating form a shell that provides formidable protection. The external shell has other advantages. One is that, because it has far more surface area than the internal skeleton found in vertebrates, it provides more points at which muscles can be attached. This increased number of muscles permits many arthropods to be stronger and more agile for their body size than birds or mammals. The coloration and markings of the exoskeleton can be beneficial as well. Many species of scorpion, for instance, have cuticles that contain hyaline. The hyaline is excited by ultraviolet radiation, so these scorpions glow blue-green when a black light is flashed on them. Scientists are not sure why scorpions have evolved to fluoresce this way, but the reason may be that their glow attracts insects that they can capture and eat.

Adaptive as their shell is, it leaves arthropods with at least one distinct disadvantage: The cuticle cannot expand to accommodate

growth. As the animal increases in size, therefore, it must occasionally molt. The existing cuticle separates from newer, more flexible layers being secreted beneath it, gradually splits open, and can be shaken or slipped off. The new chitin and protein will harden and be provided with a fresh lipid coating, but this process can take hours or days after molting occurs. The arthropod must first take in extra air or water to swell its body to greater than its normal size. After the shell has hardened in its expanded form, the arthropod expels the air or water. It then has room for growth. But until it hardens, the new coat is tender and easily penetrated. Accordingly, the arthropod must remain in hiding. Otherwise, it risks being snapped up by a predator clever enough to take advantage of its lowered defenses.

Clearly, you wouldn't approach a computer-based TOEFL reading passage in the same way that you approach a paper-based test. For one thing, you won't be able to underline, circle, or otherwise make marks on the text. (Well, you could, but the testing center probably wouldn't be happy if you ruined its computer screens!)

Also, on the computer-based TOEFL, you'll have to take each portion of the test in its entirety. In other words, you cannot skip part of the Reading section, go on to the Listening section, and then return to the Reading section; however, you can skip questions *within* certain sections of the Reading section.

The audio portions of the test are also computer based, and the speaking portion will ask you to speak into a recording device.

BEFORE WE BEGIN

Before we discuss the TOEFL, there are a few basic principles to keep in mind for any standardized, multiple-choice test.

Wrong Answers

One of the advantages of a multiple-choice test is that the answer to every question is right there on the screen! To minimize this advantage, test writers have to make the wrong answers seem correct; often, the wrong answers are particularly appealing, and test takers fall into the trap of picking answers that seem too good to be true.

Learning to recognize and avoid these trap answers is one of the keys to your success on the TOEFL. For each question in this book, be sure to review both the right and wrong answers so you have an idea of what both good and bad answers look like.

Increase Your Odds

Identifying wrong answers greatly improves your chances of getting a question correct. On the TOEFL, each multiple-choice question has four answer choices, which means you have a 25 percent (1 in 4) chance of guessing correctly. However, by using Process of Elimination (POE) to cross off wrong answers, you greatly increase your odds. (We discuss POE more in the "Reading Strategy" chapter later in this book.) Finding and eliminating just one wrong answer means you have a 33 percent (1 in 3) chance of guessing correctly, and eliminating two answers raises your odds of guessing correctly to 50 percent (1 in 2)!

REGISTERING FOR THE TOEFL

The easiest way to register for the TOEFL is online at **www.ets.org/toefl**. Because the test is Internet based, many testing times are available, although this isn't necessarily true overseas. Make sure to register early so that you receive a testing time and location with which you are comfortable.

You may take the TOEFL as many times as you like. Many programs will simply take your best score, but don't forget to check with admissions counselors from the schools to which you are applying for specific information.

WHAT IS THE PRINCETON REVIEW?

The Princeton Review is *the* premier test-preparation company; we prepare tens of thousands of students each year for tests such as the TOEFL, SAT, GMAT, GRE, LSAT, and MCAT. At the Princeton Review, we spend countless hours researching tests and figuring out exactly how to crack them. We offer students proven, high-powered strategies and techniques that help them beat the tests and achieve their best scores.

In addition to our books, we offer both live classroom instruction and online courses. If you would like more information about our programs, visit us at **PrincetonReview.com**.

If you are looking for information on Princeton Review courses offered outside the United States, go to **www.princetonreview.com/international-locations.aspx**.

Once again, for more information about all of the sections on the TOEFL, please pick up our latest edition of *Cracking the TOEFL*, in stores now.

Part II
Vocabulary
Review

Chapter 1
Introduction to Vocabulary

VOCABULARY AND THE TOEFL

Mastering vocabulary is an integral part of your success on the TOEFL. On the Reading section, it will aid in your understanding of the passage. It will also help you to identify the correct answer on vocabulary-in-context questions, which give you a word from a passage and ask you to select a synonym from four answer choices.

On the Listening section, mastering vocabulary will allow you to understand campus conversations and academic lectures more easily. Also, knowing the definition and spelling of words that you are writing down will help you to take notes quickly, instead of pondering every unknown word.

On the Speaking section, your response to the questions will be more impressive if you correctly use these vocabulary words, including accurate pronunciation. You will be judged on your use of grammar and vocabulary, as well as other factors, such as delivery. Furthermore, parts of the Speaking section require you to read and understand a passage, for which vocabulary is essential.

On the Writing section, you will again have the luxury of impressing the graders with responses that are rich in vocabulary. And, as with the Speaking section, you will have to read and understand passages, which make learning vocabulary crucial.

As you can see, every section on the TOEFL is impacted by vocabulary. Therefore, mastering these words, their definitions, and the ways in which they are used and pronounced, is an essential step in TOEFL preparation.

How We Chose These Words

We chose the 250 words commonly seen on the TOEFL. In some cases, these are not the hardest words that you will find on the TOEFL; this is intentional. Studying a hard word that was used on only one TOEFL exam and may never be used again will not help you to do better on the test. In fact, you can find endless lists online that contain incredibly difficult words that appeared on only one TOEFL exam; however, you will most likely not see any of these words when you take the test. We want you to learn words that appear often, so that when you see them, you immediately know them. Why bother learning words that won't appear on the exam? Spend your studying time and energy wisely.

Furthermore, when the test writers use an incredibly difficult word, often they will add its definition (either in parentheses or after a comma). If you have the definition in front of you, there is no need to master the word ahead of time. Therefore, studying those endless lists of incredibly challenging words will be a waste of your time as far as doing well on the test goes.

However, studying medium-level words that have been used on more than one TOEFL, and will very likely be used again, *will* help you do better on the test.

As you read through this section of the book, you may notice that some of these medium-level words look familiar; you may even believe that you know the meaning. However, before crossing off the word as "learned," you will want to be sure that you can define the word, know which part of speech it is, how to pronounce it, and how to use it in a sentence.

For instance, you've most likely seen the word "advice." But make sure that you have truly mastered it, and that you know how it differs from the word "advise." The spelling is the same, except for one letter, but the parts of speech and the meanings are different.

Truly mastering each word in this book, no matter how easy some may look, will make you more prepared for all four sections of the TOEFL on test day.

You may notice that some of the words in this book sound simple; we did this intentionally. Not only are these the words that you will encounter on the test, they are also trickier than they may seem. Though they may *sound* simple, these words are often unknowingly used incorrectly by test takers.

We have made the definitions as fundamental as possible: There's no sense in learning a word if the definition is too hard to understand and remember. You can find more complex definitions in a dictionary, but we find that this simple and straightforward approach is best, and that it makes the words easier to remember.

If you want to further expand your vocabulary, pick up the latest editions of *Word Smart* and *More Word Smart.*

Most words have second and third definitions. For the words in this book, we picked one definition—the definition that is most commonly used on the TOEFL. While you can learn additional definitions by referencing a dictionary, we have saved you the time, because the main definitions that we present are the ones you will need to know for the test.

Finally, most words have multiple forms; "reduce" can be "reducing," "reduced," and "reduces." This book presents the forms that are most commonly found on the TOEFL. If "reduced" is repeatedly used on the test, we will test you on this form of the word.

Using Notations

As we discussed in the previous section, your mission is to review these words until you know them by heart.

One device that can help you identify the words you've mastered and the words you still need to learn is to use notations. Every time you encounter a word in this book, you can make a mark to indicate your familiarity with its pronunciation, its part in speech, and its meaning; all parts are equally important. If you know the meaning of a word but can't pronounce it, that will affect your score on the Speaking section. Likewise, if you know a word's part of speech but not its meaning, you run the risk of using it incorrectly and losing points on the Writing section.

So, to remind yourself of your familiarity with each of these factors, you can make marks next to each word. For instance:

✔ means "Without a doubt, I know the pronunciation, part of speech, and meaning."

? means "I don't know this word of any of its other parts."

O means "I know one or two things, such as the pronunciation or part of speech, but I don't know other parts."

You can consider the words with check marks as words you've mastered, and you'll only need to review those words once or twice before the test. However, you'll need to continue to drill the other two categories until they fall into the check mark category. This process will save you time because the majority of your studying will be restricted to the words that you still need to learn.

PRONUNCIATION

We don't use standard dictionary phonetics in this book for the simple reason that many people don't understand phonetics. Instead, we use a modified phonetic approach that we believe is largely intuitive. The pronunciation key below should clear up any questions you may have about how to use our pronunciation guide.

The letter(s)	is (are) pronounced like the letter(s)	in the word(s)
a	a	bat, can
ah	o	con, on
aw	aw	paw, straw
ay	a	skate, rake
e	e	stem, hem, err
ee	ea	steam, clean
i	i	rim, chin, hint
ing	ing	sing, ring
oh	o	row, tow
oo	oo	room, boom
ow	ow	cow, brow
oy	oy	boy, toy
u, uh	u	run, bun
y (ye, eye)	i	climb, time
ch	ch	chair, chin
f	f, ph	film, phony
g	g	go, goon
j	j	join, jungle
k	c	cool, cat
s	s	solid, wisp
sh	sh	shoe, wish
z	z	zoo, razor
zh	s	measure

All other consonants are pronounced as you would expect. Capitalized letters are the part of the word that you pronounce with emphasis, or accent.

OTHER WAYS TO BOOST YOUR VOCABULARY

In addition to working with this book, there are other way that you can enhance your vocabulary on a daily basis; learning new words and using them correctly will be beneficial to you on every section of the TOEFL (and in real life!).

Here are some other ways you can boost your vocabulary:

- Read magazines such as *Time, Discover, Entertainment Weekly, Sports Illustrated,* and newspapers such as *USA Today* or *The New York Times.* This will help your comprehension as well as your vocabulary.
- Watch television and listen to the radio. These are enjoyable ways to learn the language! Almost any show or program will be helpful.
- Do a quick search on the Internet to find a number of helpful websites which are devoted to helping people learn English. You an even find online dictionaries with audio that will demonstrate how to pronounce new words.
- Make an effort to engage in conversation using words that you are still in the process of learning. You can even chat with people online to try out your new vocabulary.
- When you hear a word that you don't know, write it down immediately. Come back to it later and do three things:
  (1) Look up the word in the dictionary and write down on a flashcard its pronunciation, part of speech, and definition.
  (2) Make a sentence using that word.
  (3) Continue to review the flashcard until you know all the parts of your new word and can use it in a sentence.

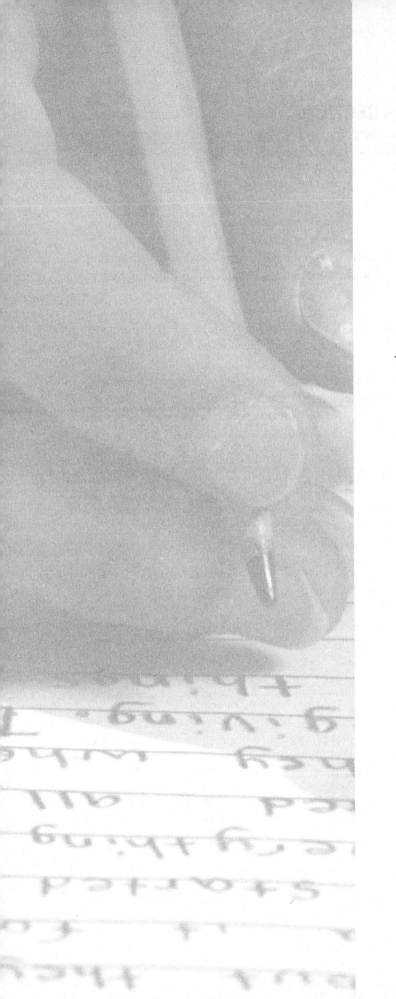

Chapter 2
Vocabulary Words
and Drills

HOW TO USE THIS SECTION

This chapter is divided into eight sections of related words. For example, the section titled "Change and Expression" is about words that have to do with changing and being different, as well as words that have to do with expressing your opinion. Each section represents a manageable set of words that can be learned as a chunk.

If you try to memorize all of these words in one sitting, it won't work. It takes time to transfer knowledge from your short-term memory to your long-term memory, so take at least three to four days to let your mind absorb the words before moving on to the next section. Occasionally, come back to a chapter you've already read to test your memory and review these words.

At the end of each section, you will find drills that quiz you on every word in the section. After doing the drills, consult the answer key to check your work.

Some of these quizzes will help you practice your speaking and writing skills. These quizzes will ask you to answer a question (either by speaking or writing) using a smaller batch of words in the section. While there are many possible answers to these questions, an answer key with sample responses has been provided for you. Another way to practice your speaking skills is to read the same responses aloud. The more you practice using these words, the more confident you are going to feel about them on test day.

CHANGE AND EXPRESSION

The following is a list of words about changing, being different, giving an opinion and winning an argument.

ADAPT (uh DAPT) v
to change in order to better handle a situation

> Even though I dislike camping the woods, I decided that the best way to *adapt* to my surroundings was to sleep in a tent instead of in my car.

ADVANTAGE (ad VAN tij) v
a benefit; a better position

> Our team had the *advantage* in the basketball game because one of our players is seven feet tall.

AFFECT (uh FEKT) v
to cause change in something

> I know that drinking coffee will *affect* my energy level, so tonight I will drink twelve cups and get all of my work done.

ALTERNATIVE (awl TUR nuh tiv) n
an option; something that you can choose instead of something else

> The heater in my house is not working, so I must use a blanket as an *alternative* way to warm myself.

APPEAL (uh PEEL) n
a request for help

> Because my grades were suffering, I made an *appeal* to my professor and asked for extra help.

ARGUE (AHR gyoo) v
to state that you agree or disagree with something

> The lawyer tried to *argue* that his client ran away because he has a phobia of police sirens.

CONFLICT (kuhn FLIKT) v
to fight; disagree

> I must point out that your arguments *conflict* with the author's thesis.

CONTRADICT (kon truh DIKT) v
to give an opposite statement

> It makes me angry when you *contradict* everything I say.

CONVINCE (kuhn VINS) v
to make someone believe in something

> Hong was able to *convince* her husband to buy a new car to match her dress.

CRITICAL (KRIT I kuhl) adj
judgemental

> The *critical* bride told her bridesmaids that their dresses were too short and told the florist that the flowers were ugly.

DIVERSITY (di VUR si tee) n
variety; a state of difference

> The *diversity* of the senior class became clear when we all chose different career paths.

ENCOURAGE (en KUR ij) v
to inspire with hope

> Lisa's boss tried to *encourage* her to take on more responsibilities by telling her she would make more money.

ENSURE (en SHOOR) v
to make sure or certain

> To *ensure* that you will remember to meet me at the basketball game tonight, I am giving you the tickets in advance.

EVOLVE (ee VAHLV) v
to develop or get better slowly

> It is true that Cro-Magnon man did not have the capacity to understand that he would *evolve* into today's human being.

EXCEPT (ik SEPT) prep
leaving out; instead of; everything but

> Unfortunately, the limousine driver was able to fit everyone in the care *except* for me, so I had to walk home.

EXPERIMENT (eks PEER un ment) n
a scientific test or trial

> The physics student described the arc of an object in flight with an *experiment* that involved a baseball.

FLUCTUATE (FLUHK choo yet) v
to change or move back and forth

> It was difficult for me to decide whether I should purchase a laptop or a desktop computer, because my needs *fluctuate*.

IMPROVE (im PROOV) v
to make better

> The professor said that I can *improve* my resume by doing an internship at a marketing firm.

INNOVATIONS (in uh VEY shuhns) n
advances or improvements in various areas of life

> Thomas Edison was responsible for many *innovations* in addition to the light bulb.

MIGRATE (MYE grayt) v
to move from one place to another

> Because they get cold up North, birds *migrate* to the South for the winter.

OPPOSE (uh POHZ) v

to go against; disagree with

> Many people *oppose* animal testing and, therefore, check the label before purchasing a bottle of shampoo.

PREVENT (pri VENT) v

to stop from happening

> The bodyguard's job was to *prevent* anyone from coming close to the president.

PROMOTE (pruh MOHT) v

to help; to speak in favor of

> The record label wanted to *promote* their new star, so they had him appear on every talk show.

PROVE (proov) v

to show to be true

> I entered a smiling contest to *prove* that I had the prettiest smile in town.

REDUCED (ri DOOSD) v

made less or smaller

> I was very excited about the sale at the university bookstore because all of the prices had been *reduced*.

REPLACED (ri PLEYSD) v

changed one with another

> Thrilled that she got her first paycheck, Cari immediately *replaced* her old cell phone with a newer model.

RESIST (ri ZIST) v

to fight against

> The criminal attempted to *resist* arrest by running away at full speed and not looking back.

TRANSFORMED (trans FOHRMD) v

changed

> David, who was unhappy with his appearance, started going to the gym and was *transformed* into someone with very large muscles.

VARY (VER ee) v

to change

> Ivan chose to *vary* his work schedule by coming in on Wednesdays instead of Fridays.

Change and Expression Drills

The answers can be found in Chapter 3.

Quiz #1

Match each word in the first column with its definition in the second column.

1.	Migrate	a.	an option, something that you can choose instead
2.	Transformed	b.	made smaller
3.	Adapt	c.	to fight against
4.	Reduced	d.	to make better
5.	Experiment	e.	to move from one place to another
6.	Evolve	f.	variety; a state of difference
7.	Vary	g.	changed
8.	Alternative	h.	changed one with another
9.	Affect	i.	advances or improvements in various areas of life
10.	Improve	j.	to cause change in something
11.	Fluctuate	k.	a scientific test or trial
12.	Resist	l.	to change or move back and forth
13.	Diversity	m.	to change
14.	Innovations	n.	to change in order to better handle a situation
15.	Replaced	o.	to develop or get better slowly

Quiz #2

Match each word in the first column with its definition in the second column.

1.	Prove	a.	to make someone believe in something
2.	Oppose	b.	to help; to speak in favor of
3.	Contradict	c.	judgmental
4.	Prevent	d.	a benefit; a better position
5.	Convince	e.	to inspire with hope
6.	Ensure	f.	to fight; disagree
7.	Conflict	g.	to make sure or certain
8.	Critical	h.	to give an opposite statement
9.	Encourage	i.	leaving out; instead of
10.	Appeal	j.	a request for help
11.	Except	k.	to go against; disagree with
12.	Argue	l.	to stop from happening
13.	Advantage	m.	to state that you agree or disagree with something
14.	Promote	n.	to show to be true

Quiz #3

Practice your essay writing skills by answering the following question in the space provided below. Use every word from this chapter in your response.

Question: Some people believe it is important to forgive and forget. Others are more likely to hold a grudge. Which approach do you think is better and why?

Use all of these words in your response.

Advantage	Appeal
Argue	Conflict
Contradict	Convince
Critical	Encourage
Ensure	Except
Oppose	Prevent
Promote	Prove

_____

_____

_____

_____

_____

_____

_____

_____

_____

_____

_____

_____

_____

REASONING AND COMPARISONS

The following is a list of words about thinking things over, comparing items, reflecting on thoughts and expressing certainty or uncertainty.

ADJACENT (uh JEY suhnt) adj
next to

> My favorite restaurant is *adjacent* to the theater, so I usually go to dinner there before seeing a movie.

ANALYSIS (uh NAL uh sis) n
a study of the basics of something

> An accountant did an *analysis* of my finances and, after looking over all the data, concluded that I am poor.

AWARE (uh WAIR) adj
having knowledge

> After thinking hard about why I did not have enough time for my schoolwork, I became *aware* that I watch too much television.

BELIEF (bi LEEF) n
an opinion; faith in something

> Most teachers hold a strong *belief* that if one reads every day, one will expand his or her vocabulary.

COMBINE (kuhm BAHYN) v
to mix together

> In science class, Julie was asked to *combine* two liquids, which led to an explosion.

COMPARE (kuhm PAIR) v
to look for or show how things are the same

> You can *compare* the wings of a plane with those of a bird because both have curved topsides and flat undersides.

CONCENTRATE (KON suhn treyt) v
to think hard about

> While taking the test, Giacomo found it easiest to *concentrate* if he put his fingers in his ears to block out all noise.

CONCEPT (KON sept) n
an idea

> Even though the professor explained the *concept* of string theory for an entire lecture, I was still confused.

CONSIDER (kuhn SID er) v
to think about something

> Before you fall in love with that painting, I think you should *consider* the large price tag on it.

CONTRAST (kuhn TRAST) v
to look for or show how things are different

> In my term paper, I decided that I would *contrast* the American Congress with the British House of Parliament because the two are different in many ways.

DECISION (di SIZH uhn) n
a final choice

> Even though he would have to dress up like a giant lizard, the movie star made the *decision* to accept the role.

DIFFERENCE (DIF er uhns) n
the state of being unlike

> The only *difference* between my twin brother and me is that I have a very large nose.

ESTIMATE (ES tuh meyt) v
to guess based on knowledge

> Based on my research, I *estimate* that a person can live without water for eleven days.

INFERRED (in FURD) v
guess based on hints

> I *inferred* from his clothes that he was a basketball player.

OBJECTIVE (uhb JEK tiv) n
a goal or purpose

> The *objective* of my presentation was to show the class how to play the drums.

OPINION (uh PIN yuhn) n
a personal view or thought

> Aggie is a connoisseur of hamburgers so, when sampling them at various restaurants, she always voices her *opinion*.

PATTERN (PAT ern) n
a specific order of things

> We are starting to notice a *pattern* to Fred's behavior because whenever he's late for work, he has a million excuses.

POSSIBILITY (pos uh BIL i tee) n
something that could happen

> I wanted to expand my dog-walking business, so I looked into the *possibility* of creating my own website.

PREFER (pri FUR) v
to like one over another

> I *prefer* to eat chicken instead of fish because I am worried about accidentally swallowing a small bone.

PROBABLY (PROB uh blee) adj
very likely

> I told my coworker that I will *probably* ride my bicycle to the office because my car is getting repaired.

REFLECTED (re FLEK tid) v
to show or think back

> To prepare herself for the upcoming race, Jodi *reflected* on her coach's words of encouragement.

RELATED (ri LEY tid) adj
having to do with something else

> The idea of my new diet is that eating pasta sauce is directly *related* to losing unwanted pounds.

RELATIVELY (REL uh tiv lee) adv
compared to something else

> Though they are both standoffish animals, the gorilla is *relatively* more friendly than the baboon.

SIMILAR (SIM uh ler) adj
alike

> Graduate school and college are *similar* in that you have to choose a field of study, do research, and often write a final paper.

SOPHISTICATED (suh FIS ti key tid) adj
having high-class tastes; cultured

> I wanted to appear more *sophisticated* at work, so I started wearing business suits and glasses.

SPECIFIC (spi SIF ik) adj
special; particular

> I pointed to the *specific* spot on the map where I wanted to spend my summer vacation—namely, Aruba.

SUFFICIENT (suh FISH uhnt) adj
enough

> Johann bought groceries on Monday, and assumed they would be *sufficient* for the week, but by Thursday his refrigerator was empty.

SURROUNDED (suh ROUND id) v
closed in on all sides

> When I went scuba diving, I was shocked and terrified to find myself *surrounded* by sharks.

THEORY (THEER ee) n
an idea that something is true

> Shannon has a *theory* that it always rains on days when she forgets her umbrella.

UNDERSTAND (uhn der STAND) v
to know what something means

> The professor asked if anyone had questions about crop rotation and because I did not *understand*, I raised my hand.

Reasoning and Comparisons Drills

The answers can be found in Chapter 3.

Quiz #1
Match each word in the first column with its definition in the second column.

1.	Belief	a.	to show or think back
2.	Analysis	b.	an idea
3.	Sophisticated	c.	to think hard about something
4.	Aware	d.	to study the basics of something
5.	Objective	e.	to guess based on hints
6.	Decision	f.	having knowledge
7.	Reflected	g.	to guess based on knowledge
8.	Understand	h.	an idea that something is true
9.	Concentrate	i.	a goal or purpose
10.	Considering	j.	to think about something
11.	Opinion	k.	an opinion; faith in something
12.	Concept	l.	to know what something means
13.	Theory	m.	a personal view or thought
14.	Estimate	n.	final choice
15.	Inferred	o.	having high-class tastes; cultured

Quiz #2
Match each word in the first column with its definition in the second column.

1.	Pattern	a.	having to do with something else
2.	Surrounded	b.	alike
3.	Prefer	c.	very likely
4.	Similar	d.	to like one over another
5.	Adjacent	e.	the state of being unlike
6.	Contrast	f.	enough
7.	Related	g.	next to
8.	Possibility	h.	to mix together
9.	Compare	i.	special; particular
10.	Sufficient	j.	a specific order of things
11.	Probably	k.	something that could be true
12.	Specific	l.	to look for or show how things are different
13.	Difference	m.	compared to something else
14.	Relatively	n.	to look for or show how things are the same
15.	Combine	o.	closed in on all sides

GROWING AND SHRINKING

This rather large list of words has to do with size, growth, and extra or excessive items.

ABSORB (ab SAWRB) v
to soak in or take in

> In order to *absorb* all the details of the story, Naylon leaned closer and gave his full attention.

ABUNDANT (uh BUHN duhnt) adj
existing in a great amount

> The taxis in New York City were *abundant*, so Rebecca easily found one to take her uptown.

ACCUMULATE (uh KYOO myuh leyt) v
to gather

> I noticed that after I hadn't cleaned my house for a month, the dust began to *accumulate*.

ADDITIONAL (uh DISH uh nl) adj
more than what is expected

> The doctor said that I should eat more vegetables, so I had an *additional* serving of green beans for dinner.

BENEFIT (BEN uh fit) n
something good

> One *benefit* of playing a musical instrument is that you can meet many people with a similar interest.

COMPLEX (kuhm PLEKS) adj
complicated

> I wanted to fix my car by myself, but I found that the inner workings were more *complex* than I originally thought.

CONSIDERABLE (kuhn SID er uh buhl) adj

large; great in amount

> I stared at my *considerable* amount of homework and started to cry.

DECLINE (di KLAHYN) v

to go downward; worsen

> We witnessed the enthusiasm of the crowd quickly *decline* when they discovered that Beyoncé was not on the premises.

DEPOSIT (di POZ it) v

to place into something

> Each night, the husband and wife *deposit* their false teeth in glasses of water.

DESTROYED (di STROID) v

torn down or ruined

> When the flood swept through town, the water leaked into our basement and *destroyed* many of our things.

DEVELOP (di VEL uhp) v

to become more advanced

> It is important for a child to share toys in order to *develop* good social skills.

DOMINANT (DOM uh nuhnt) adj

the strongest factor or person

> The Smith family likes to joke that their five-year-old daughter is the *dominant* member of the household because she always gets her way.

DRAMATIC (druh MAT ik) adj

standing out; causing strong emotion

> When the clown arrived at the birthday celebration, he made a *dramatic* entrance by running through the door and squeaking his rubber nose.

ELIMINATE (i LIM uh neyt) v
to get rid of completely

> The dentist told Peter, "If you want to *eliminate* cavities in your mouth, you have to brush your teeth every day."

EMERGE (i MURJ) v
to come out

> She was excited to *emerge* from the birthday cake and surprise him.

ESPECIALLY (i SPESH uh lee) adv
more than usual

> Donna, who has painted every room in her house, is *especially* pleased with the color in the living room.

ESSENTIAL (uh SEN shuhl) adj
needed the most; necessary

> For Sara, an *essential* part of celebrating the holidays is for everyone in her family to gather at her grandmother's house for dinner.

EXPAND (ik SPAND) v
to make broader or wider

> Ken ate ten slices of pizza and saw his stomach *expand*.

EXTREME (ik STREEM) adj
far removed from normal

> Janet found that she had an *extreme* reaction to chocolate when, after taking a bite of chocolate cake, her face swelled up.

IDEAL (ahy DEEL) adj
perfect; best

> The *ideal* way to disguise your appearance is to wear dark glasses, speak in a fake accent, and have a scarf cover your mouth.

IMITATION (im i TEY shuhn) n
a copy

> At parties, I am often asked to do my *imitation* of Elvis Presley, which makes everyone laugh.

IMPORTANT (im PAWR tnt) adj
of great meaning or consequence

> To conserve energy, it is *important* that you turn off all the lights when you leave the house.

INCREASE (in KREES) v
to make bigger

> I found that loud noises *increase* my headaches.

IRRELEVANT (i REL uh vuhnt) adj
not necessary; not related

> At the interview, Laszlo explained that he was a very good typist, but that was *irrelevant* to the job of a chef.

LACK (lak) n
an absence of something

> I couldn't contribute to my coworker's gift due to my *lack* of money.

LIMITED (LIM i tid) adj
within limits; restricted

> The professor said that he only had a *limited* amount of time to meet with me after class.

MAINLY (MEYN lee) adv
for the most part; primarily

> I've *mainly* read about Sigmund Freud, so I am interested to learn about other psychiatrists and their theories.

MAJOR (MEY jer) adj
great in size or meaning

> In poker, there is one *major* rule to follow—do not let your opponents see you sweat.

NECESSARY (NES uh ser ee) adj
needed

> It is *necessary* for me to use all of my vacation days because, if unused, I lose them at the end of the year.

OCCASIONAL (uh KEY zhuh nl) adj
happening on and off, or once in a while

> Even though I do not like sand or water, I will take an *occasional* trip to the beach about twice a year.

POROUS (POWR uhs) adj
having holes which allow liquid to go through

> The *porous* roof of the old barn allowed water to drip on the cows when it rained.

PRIMARY (PRAHY mer ee) adj
happening first; main

> Seamus admits to having many anxieties, but his *primary* fear is spiders.

PROGRESS (PROG res) n
movement forward

> Jacob could tell that he was making *progress* as a journalist when everyone complimented him on the newspaper article he had written.

PROFOUND (pruh FOUND) adj
full of knowledge; deep

> I thought it was *profound* when my philosophy professor told me, "Do or do not; there is no try."

REMAIN (ri MEYN) v
to stay in place

> Annoyed by our whispering during her lecture, the professor asked that we *remain* after class for punishment.

SEPARATE (SEP uh reyt) v
to pull apart

> By squeezing the nutcracker with all my might, I was able to *separate* the two halves of the walnut.

SIGNIFICANT (sig NIF I kuhnt) adj
worth noting; full of meaning

> A *significant* number of people who suffer from migraine headaches say that the migraines cause nausea and sensitivity to light.

STIMULATE (STIM yuh leyt) v
to bring to action

> After the markets declined, the Federal Reserve attempted to *stimulate* the economy by lowering interest rates.

SUBSTANTIAL (suhb STAN shuhl) adj
large; hard to move

> I had to stay late after work because I still had a *substantial* amount of customer phone calls to make.

UNIQUE (yoo NEEK) adj
singular; with no equal

> My upside-down house is *unique* and unlike any other house on our block.

UNUSUAL (uhn YOO zhoo uhl) adj
not expected; not normal; unfamiliar

> Lily wore an *unusual* hat with feathers, flowers, and fruit sticking out of the top.

VARIOUS (VAIR ee uhs) adj
many different things or kinds

> I am well known to the *various* groups in town, such as the Book Club and the Garden Society.

WASTE (weyst) n
something that is not needed, extra

> Max always eats every morsel on his dinner plate, because he does not want to leave any *waste*.

Growing and Shrinking Drills

The answers can be found in Chapter 3.

Quiz #1
Match each word in the first column with its definition in the second column.

1.	Deposit	a.	to make broader or wider
2.	Absorb	b.	torn down or ruined
3.	Increase	c.	to come out
4.	Destroyed	d.	movement forward
5.	Stimulate	e.	to put down into
6.	Eliminate	f.	within limits; restricted
7.	Accumulate	g.	to make bigger
8.	Expand	h.	having holes which allow liquid to go through
9.	Porous	i.	to gather
10.	Emerge	j.	to get rid of completely
11.	Decline	k.	absence of something wanted
12.	Limited	l.	to soak in or take in
13.	Develop	m.	to make something more advanced
14.	Lack	n.	to go downward
15.	Progress	o.	to bring to action

Quiz #2
Match each word in the first column with its definition in the second column.

1.	Important	a.	of great meaning or consequence
2.	Necessary	b.	great in size or meaning
3.	Especially	c.	full of knowledge; deep
4.	Profound	d.	needed the most; necessary
5.	Substantial	e.	large; great in amount
6.	Considerable	f.	happening first
7.	Ideal	g.	perfect; best
8.	Dominant	h.	standing out; causing strong emotion
9.	Major	i.	for the most part
10.	Significant	j.	needed
11.	Essential	k.	worth noting; full of meaning
12.	Primary	l.	the strongest factor or person
13.	Mainly	m.	large; hard to move
14.	Dramatic	n.	more than normally

Quiz #3

Match each word in the first column with its definition in the second column.

1.	Various	a.	a copy
2.	Complex	b.	far removed from normal
3.	Occasional	c.	singular; with no equal
4.	Abundant	d.	existing in a great amount
5.	Unique	e.	to pull apart
6.	Imitation	f.	not necessary
7.	Additional	g.	something good
8.	Separate	h.	many different things or kinds
9.	Waste	i.	to stay in place
10.	Extreme	j.	something that is not needed
11.	Benefit	k.	complicated
12.	Unusual	l.	not expected; not normal; unfamiliar
13.	Irrelevant	m.	more than what is expected
14.	Remain	n.	happening on and off or once in a while

Quiz #4

Practice your essay writing skills by answering the following question in the space provided below. Use every word from this chapter in your response.

Question: Do you agree or disagree with the following statement? You will learn all of life's most important lessons before the time you are ten years old.

Use all of these words in your response:

Considerable	Dominant
Profound	Dramatic
Especially	Essential
Ideal	Important
Mainly	Major
Necessary	Primary
Significant	Substantial

_____

_____

_____

_____

_____

_____

_____

_____

_____

_____

_____

_____

_____

LOOK WHO'S TALKING

The following is a list of words about making statements, engaging in conversation, and explaining concepts.

ADVICE (ad VAHYS) n
an opinion that is offered

> The professor offered me *advice*, telling me what to do on the class project to get an A.

ADVISE (ad VAHYZ) v
to offer information or an opinion

> In college, the administration assigned counselors to *advise* us on important decisions.

ANNOUNCEMENT (uh NOUNS muhnt) n
a public statement

> There was an *announcement* over the loudspeaker at the football stadium that warned people not to run onto the field.

CONCERNED (kuhn SURND) adj
worried

> When the gas tank indicated that it was empty, Juan quickly became *concerned* that his car could stop.

CONSISTS (kuhn SISTS) v
is made up of

> You can make delicious cookies with an amazingly simple recipe that *consists* of only sugar, eggs and butter.

CONTAINS (kuhn TEYNS) v
holds

> The jar *contains* 450 jellybeans, but I guessed 229, so I lost the contest.

DEPICT (di PIKT) v
to show in a certain way; illustrate

> In his poem "The Road Not Taken," Robert Frost's timeless words *depict* the uneasiness that an individual faces when choosing between two paths.

DESCRIBE (di SKRAHYB) v
to show with words

> Each day, the apprentice would follow his master and listen to the older gentleman *describe* the process of making the items in his shop.

DISCUSS (di SKUHS) v
to speak about with someone else

> What I like about our friendship is that we can *discuss* politics calmly instead of irrationally.

EMPHASIZE (EM fuh syz) v
to stress the importance of something

> When speaking the English language, it is customary to *emphasize* certain syllables.

ESTABLISH (i STAB lish) v
to put down a foundation for an idea

> It is crucial for me to *establish* that I am the leader of the group, otherwise everyone else will fight for power.

EXPLAIN (ik SPLEYN) v
to make clear; describe

> Before telling you about my plans to attend culinary school, I should *explain* what led me to decide that I wanted to be a chef.

EXPRESS (ik SPRES) v
to show your feelings with words

> Some people *express* their love through words, while others show their love by giving presents.

ILLUSTRATE (IL uh streyt) v
to make clear with examples

> I would appreciate it if you could *illustrate* the differences between plant and animal cells by drawing examples of each, as I am having a hard time understanding.

IMPLY (im PLAHY) v
to offer an idea without saying it directly; suggest

> He seemed to *imply* that I am unqualified for a career in finance, even though he didn't come out and say it directly.

IMPRESS (im PRES) v
to make someone feel good about you

> When Andrew applied for a job as a magician, he tried to *impress* the interviewer with his disappearing act.

INDICATE (IN di keyt) v
to point out

> When you are driving to my house, look for the stoplight which will *indicate* where you need to turn right.

INFLUENCE (in FLOO uhns) v
to affect the outcome

> The hypnotist knew that he could *influence* my actions by saying a few words and snapping his fingers.

INFORMATION (in fer MEY shuhn) n
knowledge and facts

> On Erika's trip to the national park, she visited the Tourist Center to get a packet of *information* on all the popular sites.

INTRODUCE (in truh DOOS) v

to present a person or idea to someone for the first time.

> We already covered the background of Tennessee Williams, so our literature professor will *introduce* the next topic today—Williams's most famous plays.

MAINTAIN (meyn TEYN) v

to keep in good working order

> I learned that, when I get upset, I should take deep breaths to *maintain* a sense of calm.

MENTION (MEN shuhn) v

to say briefly

> I will try to help you fix your computer, but I should *mention* that I am certainly not an expert when it comes to programming.

PROPOSED (pruh POHZD) v

offered up for discussion

> Dan *proposed* that we eat cereal for dinner because it is his favorite food.

REFERS (ri FURS) v

makes mention of

> She *refers* to me as her closest and dearest friend, even though we just met two weeks ago.

REPRESENT (ree pri ZENT) v

to stand in place of something else

> The teacher used a cantaloupe to *represent* the size of a human brain.

RESPOND (ri SPOND) v

to answer in words

> If you ask a question, please wait for me to *respond* before you interrupt with another question.

SUGGEST (suhg JEST) v
to offer an idea

> I want to *suggest* that we enforce a dress code at the office because everyone shows up in jeans and T-shirts.

SUMMARIZE (SUHM uh rahyz) v
to state the facts briefly

> The plumber explained the problems with my sink in very technical terms, so I asked him to *summarize* his findings in more basic language.

SUPPORT (suh PAWRT) v
to hold up from below; to aid by approving or favoring

> I wanted to *support* your proposition to keep the library open year round, but I felt sorry for the people who would have to work on holidays.

Look Who's Talking Drills

The answers can be found in Chapter 3.

Quiz #1

Match each word in the first column with its definition in the second column.

1.	Discuss	a.	to say briefly
2.	Contains	b.	to offer an idea
3.	Represent	c.	to stand in place of something else
4.	Concerned	d.	to show with words
5.	Mention	e.	knowledge and facts
6.	Consists	f.	holds
7.	Announcement	g.	to speak about with someone else
8.	Information	h.	makes mention of
9.	Depict	i.	is made up of
10.	Suggest	j.	offered up for discussion
11.	Describe	k.	worried
12.	Indicate	l.	to show in a certain way
13.	Refers	m.	a public statement
14.	Introduce	n.	to present a person or idea to someone for the first time
15.	Proposed	o.	to point out

Quiz #2

Match each word in the first column with it definition in the second column.

1.	Emphasize	a.	to put down a foundation for an idea
2.	Express	b.	to make clear with examples
3.	Maintain	c.	to stress the importance of something
4.	Support	d.	to affect the outcome
5.	Imply	e.	to offer an idea without saying it directly
6.	Impress	f.	to state the facts briefly
7.	Illustrate	g.	to show your feelings with words
8.	Respond	h.	to offer information or an opinion
9.	Establish	i.	to make clear
10.	Influence	j.	to keep in good working order
11.	Advice	k.	to make someone feel good about you
12.	Summarize	l.	to answer in words
13.	Advise	m.	an opinion that is offered
14.	Explain	n.	to hold up from below; to aid by approving or favoring

Quiz #3

Practice your essay writing skills by answering the following question in the space provided below. Use every word from this chapter in your response.

Question: Choose a person who you consider to be your hero and explain your choice.

Use all of these words in your response:

Advice	Advise
Emphasize	Establish
Explain	Express
Illustrate	Imply
Impress	Influence
Maintain	Respond
Summarize	Support

_____

_____

_____

_____

_____

_____

_____

_____

_____

_____

_____

_____

_____

_____

PERSONALITY TRAITS AND THE USUAL SUSPECTS

The following is a list of words relating to character or attributes and words having to do with the normal course of events.

ACCESSIBLE (ak SES uh buhl) adj
easy to get to

> The professor announced that she would make herself *accessible* by having office hours three days a week.

AVAILABLE (uh VEY luh buhl) adj
ready; free of plans

> My boss needed someone to fill in at the last minute and, luckily for him, I was *available*.

BASIC (BEY sik) adj
simple; fundamental

> One of the *basic* rules of having a dog is that you must give it exercise every day.

CAPABLE (KEY puh buhl) adj
able to handle or do something

> The captain assured us that, even though it was her first flight, she had been through training and was perfectly *capable* of providing a safe flight.

CERTAIN (SUR tn) adj
free from doubt

> The university administrator approved our proposal, so it is *certain* that we will have a blood drive on campus next semester.

COMMON (KOM uhn) adj
widespread; ordinary

> Eva asked the hairdresser for a different style that would not make her look so *common* and ordinary.

CONVENTIONAL (kuhn VEN shuh nl) adj
based on general practice

> Some people reject *conventional* medicine and prefer a more homeopathic approach to healing the body.

DIFFICULT (DIF i khult) adj
not easily done

> I thought my canoeing trip would be relaxing, but I found that it was *difficult* and exhausting to paddle back upstream.

EFFICIENT (i FISH uhnt) adj
able to get many things done with no wasted time

> Simone's friends call her *efficient* because she runs errands all over town but is never late for an appointment.

EXPENSIVE (ik SPEN siv) adj
costing a large amount of money

> If you would like to visit the greatest theme park in the world, it's not cheap—you are in for an *expensive* day of fun.

FAMILIAR (fuh MIL yer) adj
usually known

> When I was lost in the forest, I found it difficult to leave because all the paths looked *familiar*.

FUNDAMENTAL (fuhn duh MEN tl) adj
essential; basic

> As Professor Carter explained the *fundamental* ideas behind astrophysics, I tried desperately to understand.

GENERALLY (JEN er uh lee) adv
usually; ordinarily

> Stage fright is *generally* associated with fainting or forgetting one's lines.

INTERESTING (IN ter uh sting) adj
exciting, or holding one's attention

It is *interesting* to note that, although they have the same name, American and English football are very different.

INVOLVED (in VOLVD) adj
part of something; connected

Even though I went out into the quad to study, I quickly became *involved* in a baseball game.

MOTIVATION (moh tuh VEY shuhn) n
reason for doing something

Thomas Jefferson's *motivation* for writing much of the Declaration of Independence was to establish freedom from England.

OBVIOUS (OB vee uhs) adj
easily seen

I thought it was *obvious* that I was going to buy you a scarf for your birthday, so I was happy when you were genuinely surprised.

PARTICULAR (per TIK yuh ler) adj
singular or specific

I have a *particular* distaste for fish; whenever I am offered sushi I pretend that I am allergic.

PREDICTABLE (pri DIK tuh buhl) adj
able to be known ahead of time.

After visiting several different college campuses, the setup of the dorm rooms became *predictable*.

REALISTIC (ree uh LIS tik) adj
lifelike; practical

My art teacher was impressed with my *realistic* painting of a fruit bowl.

RESPONSIBLE (ri SPON suh buhl) adj
required to do something

> Because Howard accidentally left the cake out in the rain, he is *responsible* for baking a new one.

SERIOUS (SEER ee uhs) adj
showing deep thought

> The doctor determined that her stomach pains were *serious* and that they would have to remove her appendix.

STABILITY (stuh BIL i tee) n
steadiness in position

> My lack of *stability* on skis was obvious when I came flying down the mountain with my legs over my head.

SUCCESSFUL (suhk SES fuhl) adj
having a good result

> Sadly, the poet Emily Dickinson did not become *successful* until after her death when much of her writing was discovered.

SUITABLE (SOO tuh buhl) adj
fitting; appropriate

> I bought a huge leather chair which is *suitable* for my aching back.

TECHNOLOGICAL (tek nuh LOJ i kuhl) adj
relating to industry and science

> The librarian showed us the latest *technological* advancements which would make our research process easier.

TRADITIONAL (truh DISH uh nl) adj
having to do with customs that are handed down

> Before asking a woman to marry you, it is *traditional* in American culture to ask her father's permission.

TYPICALLY (TIP i kuhl lee) adv
normally

> I *typically* eat every meal in the dining hall, so if you can't find me, look there first.

UNIVERSAL (yoo nuh VUR suhl) adj
applying to all

> Miles loved his *universal* remote control because it turned on all of his gadgets at once.

USUALLY (YOO zhoo uhl lee) adv
because of habit; typically

> I *usually* read books very quickly, but I find myself moving through this 500 page novel unbelievably slowly.

Personality Traits and the Usual Suspects Drills

The answers can be found in Chapter 3.

Quiz #1
Match each word in the first column with its definition in the second column.

1.	Predictable	a.	having to do with customs that are handed down
2.	Traditional	b.	essential; basic
3.	Common	c.	usually known
4.	Generally	d.	normally
5.	Basic	e.	lifelike; practical
6.	Familiar	f.	simple; fundamental
7.	Usually	g.	applying to all
8.	Certain	h.	fitting; appropriate
9.	Universal	i.	widespread; ordinary
10.	Obvious	j.	able to be known ahead of time
11.	Fundamental	k.	easily seen
12.	Typically	l.	because of habit; typically
13.	Conventional	m.	based on general practice
14.	Realistic	n.	usually; ordinarily
15.	Suitable	o.	free from doubt

Quiz #2
Match each word in the first column with its definition in the second column.

1.	Capable	a.	not easily done
2.	Expensive	b.	ready; free of plans
3.	Motivation	c.	reason for doing something
4.	Successful	d.	steadiness in position
5.	Accessible	e.	able to get many things done with no wasted time
6.	Serious	f.	exciting or holding your attention
7.	Available	g.	easy to get to
8.	Involved	h.	relating to industry and science
9.	Difficult	i.	singular or specific
10.	Responsible	j.	able to handle or do something
11.	Technological	k.	required to do something
12.	Efficient	l.	having a good result
13.	Stability	m.	part of something; connected
14.	Particular	n.	showing deep thought
15.	Interesting	o.	costing a large amount of money

CAUSES, EFFECTS, AND ACTIONS

The following is a list of words about leading to and arriving at results as well as words about movement and activity.

ACCEPT (ak SEPT) v
to receive or agree to something

> I decided to *accept* my brother's invitation to dinner, even though I was already full from a late lunch.

APPRECIATE (uh PREE shee yet) v
to be thankful for; to value

> Emily's children show that they *appreciate* their birthday presents by saying "thank you."

ASSISTANCE (uh SIS tuhns) n
help

> Even though I'm a terrible cook, I try to offer *assistance* in the kitchen by cleaning the pots and pans.

CAUSE (kawz) n
something that leads to a result

> The *cause* of my strong odor is that I haven't showered in one week.

COMPONENT (kuhm POH nuhnt) n
one part of something larger

> An unfortunate *component* of Megan's morning routine is that she hits the "snooze" button on her alarm clock several times before getting out of bed.

CONFORM (kuhn FAWRM) v
to act the same as other people

> Rebecca doesn't like to stand out so, in order to *conform* with her classmates, she wears the same color socks that everyone else wears.

CONTRIBUTE (kuhn TRIB yoot) v
to give something

> I decided to run for president and asked everyone in town to *contribute* to my campaign.

DESIGN (di ZAHYN) v
to plan the form of something

> We asked the famous architect to *design* a small house for our pet mouse.

DEVELOPMENT (di VEL uhp muhnt) n
the process of growth

> Because of the recent economic *development*, I was able to buy a brand-new dishwasher.

EFFECT (i FEKT) n
a result

> One *effect* of only two hours of sleep is that you may have bags under your eyes.

ENGAGE (en GEYJ) v
to get the attention of someone

> In order to *engage* his audience and make them familiar with the topic, Shaker passed around a visual aid.

EXPERIENCE (ik SPEER ee uhns) n
an event or happening

> Mozart's "Clarinet Concerto" is one of my favorite pieces; I thoroughly enjoyed the *experience* of listening to the famous clarinetist play it.

FACTORS (FAK ters) n
things that lead to a result

> Two of the *factors* involved in my decision to move to the farm are that I like wearing cowboy hats and riding horses.

FORCES (fohrs) n

things that influence or control something else

> It is no secret that my parents are the *forces* behind every decision I make.

FORM (fawrm) v

to produce or make

> In art class, we learned how to *form* a piece of clay into a beautiful teapot.

IMPACT (IM pakt) n

the change made on one thing by another

> When people make mean comments, they often do not realize the *impact* of their words on other people.

INDICATOR (IN di key ter) n

a signal

> The huge thundercloud in the sky was the first *indicator* that it would rain today.

INVESTED (in VEST id) v

put money to use

> Selena *invested* in gold bars in case the economy took a downturn.

OCCUR (uh KUR) v

to happen

> I put a piece of bread in our broken toaster oven without realizing that a fire would *occur*.

ORIGINATE (uh RIJ uh neyt) v

to begin or start

> Ranjeet had trouble deciding where his trip around the world would *originate*.

PRODUCED (pruh DOOSD) v

made, manufactured

> Honey is *produced* when bees take the nectar from flowers and bring it back to their hives.

PROVIDE (pruh VAHYD) v

to make available; give

> I asked the flight attendant to *provide* me with a pillow and blanket and she kindly agreed.

PURPOSE (PUR puhs) n

why something is done or used, reason

> The *purpose* of telling ghost stories is to frighten everyone who is listening.

REASONS (REE zuhn) n

causes for a belief, action, or fact

> My *reasons* for getting a cat are that I want some company in my apartment, and I can't resist those big, beautiful eyes.

RELY (ri LAHY) v

to depend on

> I could always *rely* on my roommate to wake me up with his snoring.

REQUIRE (ri KWAHYR) v

to need

> Some people think I'm difficult because I *require* a daily foot massage.

RESULT (ri ZULT) n

something that happens because of something else, effect

> Felix hadn't skated in years and, as a *result*, slipped as soon as he stepped on the ice.

ROLE (rohl) n

a part played; a function

> My boss's *role* is to critique my daily performance, assign projects to me, and hopefully give me a raise once a year.

SETTLED (SET uhld) v

placed in order; took up residence

> In 1620, the Pilgrims *settled* near a large stone they called Plymouth Rock.

Causes, Effects, and Actions Drills

The answers can be found in Chapter 3.

Quiz #1

Match each word in the first column with its definition in the second cloumn.

1.	Forces	a.	to happen
2.	Occur	b.	the process of growth
3.	Factors	c.	a signal
4.	Cause	d.	something that leads to a result
5.	Reasons	e.	made
6.	Indicator	f.	a result
7.	Role	g.	causes for a belief, action, or fact
8.	Development	h.	something that happens because of something else
9.	Effect	i.	things that lead to a result
10.	Impact	j.	a part played; a function
11.	Result	k.	the change made on one thing by another
12.	Produced	l.	one part of something larger
13.	Component	m.	why something is done or used
14.	Purpose	n.	things that influence or control something else

Quiz #2

Match each word in the first column with its definition in the second column.

1.	Conform	a.	to produce or make
2.	Originate	b.	to be thankful for; to value
3.	Accept	c.	help
4.	Form	d.	to receive or agree to something
5.	Settled	e.	an event or happening
6.	Provide	f.	to give something
7.	Appreciate	g.	to depend on
8.	Design	h.	to act the same as other people
9.	Engage	i.	put money to use
10.	Assistance	j.	to make available
11.	Require	k.	placed in order; took up residence
12.	Contribute	l.	to plan the form of something
13.	Rely	m.	to begin or start
14.	Experience	n.	to need
15.	Invested	o.	to get the attention of someone

Quiz #3

Practice your essay writing skills by answering the following question in the space provided below. Use every word from this chapter in your response.

Question: Do you think that a student should challenge her grades if she thinks they are unfair, or should she always assume that her teachers' grading systems are fair and accurate?

Use all of these words in your respose:

Cause   Indicator
Component   Occur
Development   Produced
Effect   Purpose
Factors   Reasons
Forces   Result
Impact   Role

_____

_____

_____

_____

_____

_____

_____

_____

_____

_____

_____

_____

_____

THE NATURAL WORLD

The following is a list of words about the living things around us and sight and observation.

AESTHETICS (es THET iks) n
visual beauty

> Kristina asked her husband to shave his beard in order to preserve the *aesthetics* of their family portrait.

APPEAR (uh PEER) v
to come into view

> I granted an interview to a reporter who told me that I would *appear* on the evening news.

BEHAVIOR (bee HEYV yer) n
someone's way of acting

> Paul's *behavior* at the party showed that he was tired, so no one was surprised when he went to bed early.

CLASSIFIED (KLAS uh fahyd) v
fit into a category

> I mistakenly *classified* Jane Austen as a historian, but my professor reminded me that she was a British novelist.

CLEARLY (KLEER lee) adv
easily seen

> Elizabeth was driving home in the dark and turned on her headlights to see *clearly*.

CLIMATE (KLAHY mit) n
weather

> San Diego, a city that is often admired for its *climate*, remains sunny year round.

CONDITIONS (kuhn DISH uhns) n
things that are needed; factors

> I need three *conditions* to maintain my happiness: chocolate, roses, and jewelry.

CULTURAL (KUHL cher uhl) adj
referring to the qualities of a civilization

> The artist Andy Warhol had a *cultural* impact on society when he added his unique twist to the Pop Art genre.

DISCOVERED (di SKUHV erd) v
came upon; learned

> While hiking in the woods, Sandra turned over a rock and *discovered* a treasure box hidden underneath.

DISPLAY (di SPLEY) v
to show

> I decided to *display* my homemade jewelry outside our university's dining hall, in hopes that others students would want to purchase something.

ENVIRONMENT (en VAHY ruhn muhnt) n
surroundings; settings

> When I am stressed out I go to the yoga studio, which is my favorite *environment* for relaxation.

EXIST (ig ZIST) v
to live; to be

> If he lived on Mars, he would have to *exist* on carbon dioxide.

EXPOSED (ik SPOHZD) adj
uncovered; open to view

> I don't know much about history, so I was embarrassed that my ignorance was *exposed* when the professor asked me to tell the class about Napoleon.

FEATURES (FEE chers) n
parts of someone's or something's appearance

> One of the amazing *features* of the blue whale is that it is bigger than any animal on earth, including many extinct dinosaurs.

FOCUS (FOH kuhs) v
to make clearer; to concentrate

> Some people call me a procrastinator because, before doing my homework, I *focus* on cleaning my room from top to bottom.

HABITAT (HAB i tat) n
a place for living

> My permanent *habitat* is on the couch, watching TV and eating potato chips.

IDENTIFY (ahy DEN tuh fahy) v
to point out

> The policeman asked me to *identify* the person who stole my purse, and I pointed to the woman on the left.

INDIVIDUAL (in duh VIJ oo uhl) n
something that stands alone

> Because I don't like working in groups, the professor allowed me to complete the project not with others, but as an *individual*.

INHABITED (in HAB i tid) v
lived in

> The forest moon of Endor is *inhabited* by furry aliens called Ewoks.

OBSERVE (uhb ZURV) v
to see or watch

> As part of my biology project, I had to *observe* a family of rats for five hours each day.

DATA AND EXPERIMENTS

The following is a list of words relating to math, science and time.

ACCURATE (AK yer it) adj
without errors

> Everyone complimented me on my performance in the game of darts because my shots were *accurate*.

APPROACH (uh PROHCH) n
a way of doing something

> My *approach* to cleaning the tiger's cage is to be very quiet.

ASSUMPTION (uh SUHMP shuhn) n
a guess

> My *assumption* that watering my plants every day would make them grow faster was proven incorrect when they died from too much moisture.

APPROXIMATELY (uh PROK suh mit lee) adv
close to; about

> Jane has *approximately* thirty minutes to eat lunch when she's rushing between classes.

CEASED (seesd) v
stopped

> When we gave the children ice cream, they immediately *ceased* crying.

CONTEMPORARY (kuhn TEM puh rer ee) adj
modern; happening at the same time

> Because we're a *contemporary* couple, I proposed to my husband instead of the other way around.

PERSPECTIVE (per SPEK tiv) n
a way of seeing; point of view

> When I sit in the passenger seat instead of the driver's seat, my *perspective* changes.

PORTRAYED (pawr TREYD) v
represented with pictures, words, or actions

> The actor, who *portrayed* Marilyn Monroe in the play, was embarrassed when he had to wear a dress.

PRESENCE (PREZ uhns) n
state of being somewhere

> My ex-boyfriend's *presence* at the party made me uncomfortable, so every time he came near, I headed in the other direction.

REALIZE (REE uh lahyz) v
to understand clearly what you hadn't before

> I didn't *realize* that I passed the exit on the highway until it was too late.

RITUAL (RICH oo uhl) n
a ceremony or an act that repeats often

> My daily morning *ritual* is to brush my teeth, wash my face, and watch the news.

SITUATION (sich oo EY shuhn) n
something's place compared to other things; circumstance

> Eric found himself in an awkward *situation* when he walked into the women's restroom by mistake.

SPECIES (SPEE sheez) n
a single class of plants or animals

> While walking along the beach, we discovered a new *species* of animal with a body like a kangaroo and a head like a fish.

STRUCTURE (STRUHK cher) n
the way something is built

> The building's *structure* was weak, so it swayed with the force of the strong winds.

SURPRISED (ser PRAHYZD) v
to come upon suddenly

> I was *surprised* to learn that Abraham Lincoln, the sixteenth president of the United States, kept important papers inside his famous top hat.

VISUAL (VIZH oo uhl) adj
having to do with sight

> I found out that I am a *visual* learner, which means that I learn best when professors use the blackboard.

The Natural World Drills

The answers can be found in Chapter 3.

Quiz #1
Match each word in the first column with its definition in the second column.

1.	Exist	a.	referring to the qualities of a civilizatio
2.	Ritual	b.	a ceremony or an act that repeats ofte
3.	Habitat	c.	parts of someone's appearance
4.	Individual	d.	the way something is built
5.	Cultural	e.	surroundings; settings
6.	Classified	f.	a single class of plants or animals
7.	Structure	g.	something that stands alone
8.	Situation	h.	lived in
9.	Behavior	i.	someone's way of acting
10.	Environment	j.	weather
11.	Features	k.	to live; to be
12.	Inhabited	l.	fit into a category
13.	Species	m.	things that are needed; factors
14.	Climate	n.	a place for living
15.	Conditions	o.	something's place compared to other things

Quiz #2
Match each word in the first column with its definition in the second column.

1.	Perspective	a.	state of being somewhere
2.	Clearly	b.	to come into view
3.	Display	c.	represented with pictures, words, or actions
4.	Realize	d.	to show
5.	Visual	e.	the study of beauty
6.	Appearance	f.	uncovered; open to view
7.	Identify	g.	a way of seeing; point of view
8.	Observe	h.	to point out
9.	Aesthetics	i.	to make clearer; to concentrate
10.	Discovered	j.	to come upon suddenly
11.	Portrayed	k.	to understand clearly what you hadn't before
12.	Presence	l.	having to do with sight
13.	Surprised	m.	to see or watch
14.	Exposed	n.	easily seen
15.	Focus	o.	came upon; learned

PERSPECTIVE (per SPEK tiv) n
a way of seeing; point of view

> When I sit in the passenger seat instead of the driver's seat, my *perspective* changes.

PORTRAYED (pawr TREYD) v
represented with pictures, words, or actions

> The actor, who *portrayed* Marilyn Monroe in the play, was embarrassed when he had to wear a dress.

PRESENCE (PREZ uhns) n
state of being somewhere

> My ex-boyfriend's *presence* at the party made me uncomfortable, so every time he came near, I headed in the other direction.

REALIZE (REE uh lahyz) v
to understand clearly what you hadn't before

> I didn't *realize* that I passed the exit on the highway until it was too late.

RITUAL (RICH oo uhl) n
a ceremony or an act that repeats often

> My daily morning *ritual* is to brush my teeth, wash my face, and watch the news.

SITUATION (sich oo EY shuhn) n
something's place compared to other things; circumstance

> Eric found himself in an awkward *situation* when he walked into the women's restroom by mistake.

SPECIES (SPEE sheez) n
a single class of plants or animals

> While walking along the beach, we discovered a new *species* of animal with a body like a kangaroo and a head like a fish.

STRUCTURE (STRUHK cher) n
the way something is built

> The building's *structure* was weak, so it swayed with the force of the strong winds.

SURPRISED (ser PRAHYZD) v
to come upon suddenly

> I was *surprised* to learn that Abraham Lincoln, the sixteenth president of the United States, kept important papers inside his famous top hat.

VISUAL (VIZH oo uhl) adj
having to do with sight

> I found out that I am a *visual* learner, which means that I learn best when professors use the blackboard.

The Natural World Drills

The answers can be found in Chapter 3.

Quiz #1
Match each word in the first column with its definition in the second column.

1.	Exist	a.	referring to the qualities of a civilization
2.	Ritual	b.	a ceremony or an act that repeats often
3.	Habitat	c.	parts of someone's appearance
4.	Individual	d.	the way something is built
5.	Cultural	e.	surroundings; settings
6.	Classified	f.	a single class of plants or animals
7.	Structure	g.	something that stands alone
8.	Situation	h.	lived in
9.	Behavior	i.	someone's way of acting
10.	Environment	j.	weather
11.	Features	k.	to live; to be
12.	Inhabited	l.	fit into a category
13.	Species	m.	things that are needed; factors
14.	Climate	n.	a place for living
15.	Conditions	o.	something's place compared to other things

Quiz #2
Match each word in the first column with its definition in the second column.

1.	Perspective	a.	state of being somewhere
2.	Clearly	b.	to come into view
3.	Display	c.	represented with pictures, words, or actions
4.	Realize	d.	to show
5.	Visual	e.	the study of beauty
6.	Appearance	f.	uncovered; open to view
7.	Identify	g.	a way of seeing; point of view
8.	Observe	h.	to point out
9.	Aesthetics	i.	to make clearer; to concentrate
10.	Discovered	j.	to come upon suddenly
11.	Portrayed	k.	to understand clearly what you hadn't before
12.	Presence	l.	having to do with sight
13.	Surprised	m.	to see or watch
14.	Exposed	n.	easily seen
15.	Focus	o.	came upon; learned

DATA AND EXPERIMENTS

The following is a list of words relating to math, science and time.

ACCURATE (AK yer it) adj
without errors

> Everyone complimented me on my performance in the game of darts because my shots were *accurate*.

APPROACH (uh PROHCH) n
a way of doing something

> My *approach* to cleaning the tiger's cage is to be very quiet.

ASSUMPTION (uh SUHMP shuhn) n
a guess

> My *assumption* that watering my plants every day would make them grow faster was proven incorrect when they died from too much moisture.

APPROXIMATELY (uh PROK suh mit lee) adv
close to; about

> Jane has *approximately* thirty minutes to eat lunch when she's rushing between classes.

CEASED (seesd) v
stopped

> When we gave the children ice cream, they immediately *ceased* crying.

CONTEMPORARY (kuhn TEM puh rer ee) adj
modern; happening at the same time

> Because we're a *contemporary* couple, I proposed to my husband instead of the other way around.

CONTINUE (kuhn TIN yoo) v
to go on after stopping

> After putting out a small fire in the kitchen, I decided to *continue* eating dinner.

CRITERIA (krahy TEER ee uh) n
factors for judgement

> When searching for a babysitter, we were looking for two *criteria*—a kind personality and driver's license.

CURRENT (KUR uhnt) adj
happening now

> I read the newspaper every day so that I can stay informed about *current* events.

DETERMINE (di TUR min) v
to decide

> The horse race was so close that we had to watch a playback of the video to *determine* the winner.

ELEMENTS (EL uh muhnts) n
parts of a whole

> The physics experiment required the following *elements*: weights, a pulley, and rope.

EVENTUALLY (I VEN choo uh lee) adv
at some time in the future

> After seven long days in the desert, the explorer was relieved when he *eventually* found water.

EVIDENCE (EV i dehns) n
the thing that proves something else

> The jury decided the man was guilty after seeing the most important piece of *evidence*: a broken guitar.

FREQUENTLY (FREE kwuhnt lee) adv
often

> Gene *frequently* eats peanut butter and marshmallow sandwiches because they are his favorite.

GRADUAL (GRAJ oo uhl) adv
slow

> My climb up the mountain was at a *gradual* pace because I was carrying a fifty-pound backpack.

IMMEDIATELY (i MEE dee it lee) adv
now; at once; right away

> When my friend told me I had spaghetti sauce all over my face, I *immediately* reached for a napkin.

INEVITABLE (in EV I tuh buhl) adj
sure to happen

> It is *inevitable* that when I study hard for a test, I will receive a better grade than if I hadn't studied at all.

METHODS (METH uhds) n
ways of doing

> There are many *methods* to cooking an egg: scramble, fry, or hard boil it.

OBTAINED (uhb TEYND) v
gathered

> I *obtained* my recommendations for graduate school and included them in my admissions envelope.

PROCESS (PROS es) n
steps for doing

> The science teacher demonstrated the *process* of turning solid gold into a liquid.

PROJECT (PROJ ekt) n
a task; plan

> To prepare a presentation about customer service, I was forced to work on a joint *project* with a coworker that I didn't like.

RANGE (reynj) n
the extent or amount of something

> On any given day, Cassandra's emotions *range* from incredibly happy to very sad.

RAPID (RAP id) adj
happening quickly

> Because I hadn't been washing my face every day, the dermatologist noticed a *rapid* decline in the health of my skin.

RARELY (RAIR lee) adv
not often; seldom

> Shirley *rarely* performs this song, so when we asked her to sing, she forgot the lyrics.

RECENTLY (REE suhnt lee) adv
not long ago

> Because it had snowed *recently*, the sidewalks were slippery.

RESEARCH (ree SURCH) v
to search for information

> I spent all day in the library doing *research* on William Shakespeare for my English class.

SCHEDULE (SKEJ ool) n
a list of activities or plans

> Kay wanted to pull her hair out in frustration because her busy *schedule* did not allow time for relaxation.

TECHNIQUE (tek NEEK) n

method of performance, procedure by which a task is accomplished

My tennis game finally improved when I mastered the *technique* of serving.

TERM (turm) n

a part of the school year or a limited period of time; also, a word used for a particular thing

At the end of the *term* I graduated, which is another *term* for finishing school.

VALUE (VAL yoo) n

the importance or worth assigned to something

One number that I can never forget is the estimated *value* of pi: 3.14.

Data and Experiments Drills

The answers can be found in Chapter 3.

Quiz #1
Match each word in the first column with its definition in the second column.

1. Project
2. Value
3. Methods
4. Approach
5. Research
6. Accurate
7. Process
8. Criteria
9. Evidence
10. Technique
11. Range
12. Assumption
13. Elements
14. Determined
15. Obtained

a. a way of doing; method of performance
b. factors for judgment
c. to search for information
d. the importance or worth assigned to something
e. the extent of something
f. gathered
g. to decide
h. a way of doing something
i. does not have errors
j. parts of a whole
k. a task; plan
l. a guess
m. ways of doing
n. the thing that proves something else
o. steps for doing a task

Quiz #2
Match each word in the first column with its definition in the second column.

1. Contemporary
2. Inevitable
3. Recently
4. Eventually
5. Gradual
6. Approximately
7. Term
8. Current
9. Schedule
10. Ceased
11. Rarely
12. Frequently
13. Immediately
14. Continue
15. Rapid

a. sure to happen
b. a list of activities or plans
c. close to
d. often
e. happening now
f. modern; happening at the same time
g. happening quickly
h. stopped
i. not often; seldom
j. slow
k. to go on after stopping
l. a part of the school year; also another word for something else
m. now; at once
n. not long ago
o. at some time in the future

Quiz #3

Practice your essay writing skills by answering the following question in the space provided below. Use every word from this chapter in your response.

Question: Agree or disagree with the following statement: If someone is given one million dollars, he or she should save the money instead of spending it.

Use all of these words in your response:

Approximately   Ceased
Contemporary   Continue
Current   Eventually
Frequently   Gradual
Immediately   Inevitable
Rapid   Rarely
Recently   Schedule
Term

_____

_____

_____

_____

_____

_____

_____

_____

_____

_____

_____

_____

_____

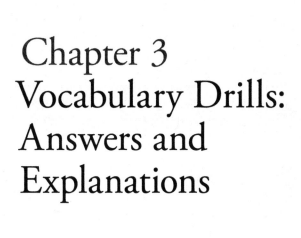

Chapter 3
Vocabulary Drills:
Answers and
Explanations

CHANGE AND EXPRESSION DRILLS

Quiz #1

1. e
2. g
3. n
4. b
5. k
6. o
7. m
8. a
9. j
10. d
11. l
12. c
13. f
14. i
15. h

Quiz #2

1. n
2. k
3. h
4. l
5. a
6. g
7. f
8. c
9. e
10. j
11. i
12. m
13. d
14. b

Quiz #3

There are many possible responses to this task. Here is a sample response.

I would have to **argue** that, if someone has wronged you in the past, you should forgive and forget instead of holding a grudge. There are many reasons for my opinion. First, your kindness would **encourage** the other person to **prevent** any wrongdoings in the future. Also, it would **ensure** that this person learns from his or her mistakes and would **promote** a sense of knowing what is right and wrong.

However, someone who would **oppose** the belief that you should forgive and forget would **contradict** my opinion and try to **convince** you that people never change, **except** in rare circumstances. This **critical** approach to the question would **conflict** with my theory that there is an **advantage** to showing others what is right and wrong.

Though I can **prove** that my approach is more beneficial because I have saved many friendships by forgiving and forgetting wrongdoings. So I would like to **appeal** to those who disagree with me and request they try to at least consider my point of view.

REASONING AND COMPARISONS DRILLS

Quiz #1
1. k
2. d
3. o
4. f
5. i
6. n
7. a
8. l
9. c
10. j
11. m
12. b
13. h
14. g
15. e

Quiz #2
1. j
2. o
3. d
4. b
5. g
6. l
7. a
8. k
9. n
10. f
11. c
12. i
13. e
14. m
15. h

GROWING AND SHRINKING DRILLS

Quiz #1
1. e
2. l
3. g
4. b
5. o
6. j
7. i
8. a
9. h
10. c
11. n
12. f
13. m
14. k
15. d

Quiz #2
1. a
2. j
3. n
4. c
5. m
6. e
7. g
8. l
9. b
10. k
11. d
12. f
13. i
14. h

Quiz #3
1. h
2. k
3. n
4. d
5. c
6. a
7. m
8. e
9. j
10. b
11. g
12. l
13. f
14. i

Quiz #4:

There are many possible responses to this task. Here is a sample response.

I disagree with the statement that you learn all of life's most important lessons by the time you are ten years old. This is a **profound** thought, but it is not accurate, especially in my case. While it would have been **ideal** to learn all of my lessons early, I am well over ten years old and still have a **considerable** amount to learn.

For instance, it is **especially essential** for me to learn my place in society, a lesson with which I still struggle. Am I a **dominant** person, who is destined to move quickly up the ladder of success? Or am I a more reserved person, who will have a slower but just as **important** road to the top? The next few years of my life will reveal these answers.

Also, I am still lacking in the **necessary** knowledge that I need in order to control my financial situation. Luckily, my **primary** income is **substantial** but, once I receive my paycheck, I don't know how to save or invest those funds. If I incorrectly manage my money, that could have a **dramatic** effect on my financial future.

Finally, while I mastered the more simple life lessons such as being selfless and caring for others, I missed out on one **major** lesson—how to tactfully say "no" when I don't want to do something. This simple rule has had a **significant** impact on my life because I end up doing favors that people have come to expect instead of appreciate. I ought to learn this lesson in the next few years or else I will be living my life **mainly** for others instead of for myself.

LOOK WHO'S TALKING DRILLS

Quiz #1

1. g
2. f
3. c
4. k
5. a
6. i
7. m
8. e
9. l
10. b
11. d
12. o
13. h
14. n
15. j

Quiz #2

1. c
2. g
3. j
4. n
5. e
6. k
7. b
8. l
9. a
10. d
11. m
12. f
13. h
14. i

Quiz #3:

There are many possible responses to this task. Here is a sample response.

My hero is my friend, Dan, for several reasons, which I will **explain**.

First, I must **establish** that he is exceedingly kind and compassionate. Most people posses some form of these traits, but it is rare to meet someone who embodies them without reservation. I cannot **emphasize** enough how caring he is.

Second, he is humble. While other people attempt to constantly **impress** everyone around them, he tries to **maintain** a level head. To **illustrate** his humility, I must mention that he received an award which he didn't tell anyone about, for fear that it would alienate others who did not receive the same recognition.

Third, he is a master of **advice**. I always turn to him when I need someone to **advise** me on many of life's important decisions. In turn, he will **express** his opinion and **imply** that I can consider his response and then form my own conclusion. He also does not **respond** with strict instructions that I must follow his advice to the letter, which I appreciate.

To **summarize**, Dan is my hero because he is kind, humble, and a master of advice. It is wonderful to have someone like him **support** me in life. And, fortunately, his **influence** has made me a better person.

PERSONALITY TRAITS AND THE USUAL SUSPECTS DRILLS

Quiz #1

1. j
2. a
3. i
4. n
5. f
6. c
7. l
8. o
9. g
10. k
11. b
12. d
13. m
14. e
15. h

Quiz #2

1. j
2. o
3. c
4. l
5. g
6. n
7. b
8. m
9. a
10. k
11. h
12. e
13. d
14. i
15. f

CAUSES, EFFECTS, AND ACTIONS DRILLS

Quiz #1

1. n
2. a
3. i
4. d
5. g
6. c
7. j
8. b
9. f
10. k
11. h
12. e
13. l
14. m

Quiz #2

1. h
2. m
3. d
4. a
5. k
6. j
7. b
8. l
9. o
10. c
11. n
12. f
13. g
14. e
15. i

Quiz #3:

There are many possible responses to this task. Here is a sample response.

The **role** of every student is to question. Therefore, I think that students are justified in challenging their grades, regardless of the **factors** involved.

One **indicator** of an unfair grade is if the student studied very hard for a test and still did not do well. The **impact** of this setback could be devastating to a hardworking student. She is left wondering, "What is the **cause** of this poor grade when I studied so hard?" If she does not challenge the grade, that question will go unanswered.

Another example of an instance in which a student should challenge a grade is if he writes a paper that was poorly received but he was proud of. In his mind, he **produced** a masterpiece. So he is left asking, "How could this possibly **occur**?" He should ask the teacher about the **forces** behind her reasoning. He should ask if there was one **component** that lead to this grade, or if his entire paper was off the mark. His **development** as a student depends on these answers.

In conclusion, a student may have many valid **reasons** to challenge a grade and, as a **result**, the teacher should always take her seriously. Poor grades can have a devastating **effect** on a student, so it is essential that she always finds out the reasoning behind the grade. Because if a student's job is to question, and she does not fulfill that job, then she has no **purpose**.

THE NATURAL WORLD DRILLS

Quiz #1

1. k
2. b
3. n
4. g
5. a
6. l
7. d
8. o
9. i
10. e
11. c
12. h
13. f
14. j
15. m

Quiz #2

1. g
2. n
3. d
4. k
5. l
6. b
7. h
8. m
9. e
10. o
11. c
12. a
13. j
14. f
15. i

DATA AND EXPERIMENTS DRILLS

Quiz #1

1. k
2. d
3. m
4. h
5. c
6. i
7. o
8. b
9. n
10. a
11. e
12. l
13. j
14. g
15. f

Quiz #2

1. f
2. a
3. n
4. o
5. j
6. c
7. l
8. e
9. b
10. h
11. i
12. d
13. m
14. k
15. g

Quiz #3

There are many possible responses to this task. Here is a sample response.

I disagree with the idea that if someone is given one million dollars he or she should save the money. That should only be the last step. In fact, if I were given one million dollars, I would first travel and shop. Only after spending half of my money would I start saving.

First, I would like to travel, which would be convenient because my **current** school **term** is coming to a close. I have **recently** become aware that there are several places around the world that I would like to visit, such as Costa Rica, Hawaii, Ireland, and Kenya. If I were given the money to travel, I would start in Costa Rica and **continue** along to the other destinations at a **gradual** pace. It is **inevitable** that after visiting these wonderful locales, I may never want to return home!

The second thing I would do with my money is shop. I can already picture myself in a **rapid** race around the shopping mall, grabbing everything in sight. I **rarely** have enough money to splurge on expensive clothes, so I would **immediately** head to my favorite stores. In my happy state, I would purchase the most **contemporary** outfits and **frequently** return to the mall to update my wardrobe.

Finally, when I **ceased** my frantic **schedule** of nonstop spending, I would start saving. I would put **approximately** half of my one million away in the bank and then continue splurging with whatever was left over. If I did not make this decision, I would **eventually** be left penniless.

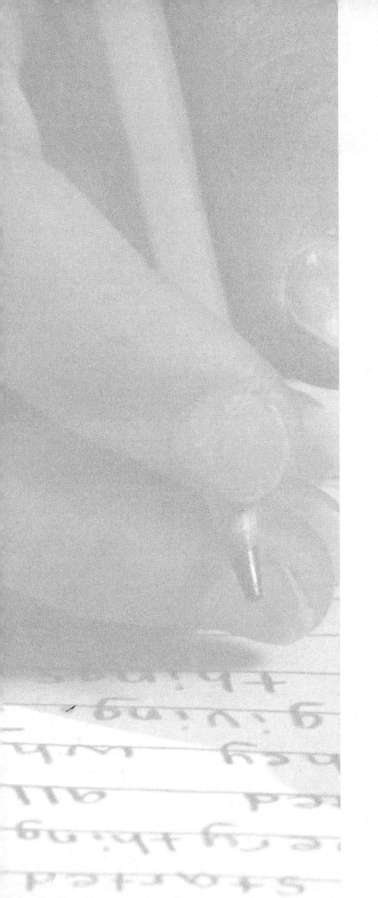

Part III
Reading
Review

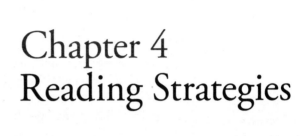

Chapter 4
Reading Strategies

The TOEFL Reading section consists of

> Three to four **passages**, each approximately 700 words long
>
> - Each passage is followed by about 12 to 14 questions
> - You will have 60 to 80 minutes to complete the entire section

As mentioned in the introduction, many of the questions are multiple choice and worth one point each, but some questions are worth two or more points. Typically, questions that are worth more appear at the end of the section.

Some of the words and phrases in the reading passages are underlined in blue on the screen; if you click on these phrases, a definition is provided. You can see what the screen will look like in the picture on the opposite page.

During the actual test, some very difficult words will appear underlined in the reading passages. The TOEFL will give you a definition of these words, so don't worry when you see them!

In the following passage, if you click on the words *uranium isotope* or *moniker*, you will see a definition of the word in question. You'll also notice that some of the words appear in gray boxes. These words have a special type of question associated with them, which we'll look at soon.

Remember, if you prefer, you are free to skip questions within this section; simply click on the "Next" button on the top right-hand side of the screen. You can return to questions you've skipped when you are ready. You can also click the "Review" button to see a display of all the questions you've answered and left blank. From this screen, you can return to any question.

TOEFL Reading

Question 3 of 12

REVIEW   HELP   BACK   NEXT
?

PAUSE   SECTION
TEST   EXIT

HIDE TIME   00:08:45

More Available

→ Although Otto Hahn and Fritz Strassmann discovered the process of nuclear fission in 1938, it took another year for scientists to truly understand the process. During this process, a <u>uranium isotope</u> is split by firing neutrons at it. When the neutron strikes the isotope, it ejects neutrons of its own, which in turn strike other uranium atoms. This sets off a chain reaction, with each split atom causing another atom to break up as well. When controlled, this type of chain reaction can be harnessed to produce useful nuclear energy. But if the reaction is not controlled, the result is far more devastating: a nuclear explosion.

→ Shortly after the discovery of the potential destructiveness of nuclear power, President Franklin Roosevelt set up a committee to investigate the feasibility of a nuclear weapon. Although initial progress was slow, the program was reorganized in 1942 under the <u>moniker</u> the Manhattan Engineer District, or simply the Manhattan Project. The project was headed by Robert Oppenheimer and was authorized to call on the full resources of the government and military to achieve its goal.

STRATEGIES FOR THE READING SECTION

Basic Principle #1: It's in There!

The first and most important principle to the Reading section is a simple one.

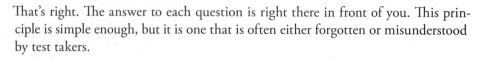

> **The answer to every single question is found in the passage!**

That's right. The answer to each question is right there in front of you. This principle is simple enough, but it is one that is often either forgotten or misunderstood by test takers.

A complete guide to the Reading Section can be found in *Cracking the TOEFL iBT.*

On the TOEFL Reading section, you are not expected to give your interpretation of what you've read. You are not required to analyze what you've read. All you're asked to do is simply *find the best answer* to the question in the passage or, in some cases, infer what *must be true* based on information provided in the passage.

Of course, this is very different from what you are used to doing in a more academic setting. The Reading section can be difficult for test takers who think too much beyond what is written in the passage. When completing the reading exercises in this book, pay careful attention to the approach used and the explanation for why the correct answer is correct.

Basic Principle #2: The Two-Pass System

Time is one of the largest barriers to your success on the TOEFL Reading section. You have only 60 minutes to read three passages and answer 36 questions. And although the majority of the questions are worth one point each, the questions are *not* equally difficult. Some question types are inherently faster or easier, whereas others will take more time or are more difficult.

Because your only goal is to get as many points as possible, it makes no sense to spend time on difficult questions when an easier question may be a click away. When we discuss the question types later in this chapter, we'll let you know which types tend to be easier. In addition, as you practice, you'll get a feel for the types of questions you can do most quickly. Make sure to seek these questions out: *Do them first* and save the killer questions for later.

Basic Principle #3: Process of Elimination

POE: Part I

Even though the right answer is found somewhere in the text, the TOEFL Reading section is still very difficult. Why? Because the other answer choices are often very tempting. Many questions include trap answers—answer choices that look correct but are actually incorrect.

To do well on the Reading section, you must use Process of Elimination, or POE. Simply put, POE involves comparing answer choices and finding reasons to eliminate one or more. POE requires you to be aggressive and get rid of many of the answer choices! Because the majority of the questions have only four choices, eliminating even one answer greatly increases your odds of getting a question correct if you are forced to guess. When using POE, make sure you examine each answer choice carefully. *Never* blindly pick the first answer that stands out or seems good, because it may be a trap!

Let's look at a sample question and see an example of how to use POE. On the test, you won't see the answer choices as letters, but we'll use them in this book to make the explanations clearer.

1. The word feasibility as used in the passage is closest in meaning to

   (A) appropriateness
   (B) reasonableness
   (C) possibility
   (D) viability

This question is based on an earlier reading passage, but that is actually not important right now. We are only concerned with the answer choices. When using POE, use your scratch paper to write "a," "b," "c," "d", and then make a mark next to each answer, based on your impression of it. Some possibilities are listed below.

Symbol	Meaning
✓	Good or okay answer
~	Weak answer
?	Unknown answer
✓✓	Best answer
X	Bad answer

Don't waste time writing down the whole question and complete answer choices. We have copied the whole question here for purposes of illustrating our point. On the actual test you should try to write down a paraphrased version of the question and answer choices.

For the example above, we may mark our scrap paper in the following way:

1. The word feasibility as used in the passage is closest in meaning to

    X   (A)   appropriateness
    ~   (B)   reasonableness
    ✓   (C)   possibility
    ?   (D)   viability

So in this case, even if we can't decide which answer is the "best" one, we can see that one of the choices is definitely out. And because we like the third answer, we may as well eliminate the "weak" answer too. That leaves us with the third and fourth answer choices. In this case, the third choice looks OK, whereas the fourth choice is a bit of a mystery.

On the TOEFL, there will be times when you're unsure of a choice. The answer may contain difficult vocabulary words or be hard to follow. Never eliminate an answer just because you don't understand it. Instead, mark it as "unknown," and check the other choices. If the remaining choices are no good, then the "unknown" choice must be correct. If one of the other choices seems more likely, then go with that one.

We'll talk more about what to do when you are stuck or down to two choices when we look at the different question types.

POE: Part II

The second part of POE is the ability to recognize the types of wrong answers found on the TOEFL. The wrong answers have to be tempting enough for you to want to pick them, but not right enough to be the best answer. In general, the wrong answers on the TOEFL Reading section fall into one of the following categories:

- **Not mentioned:** This category consists of information that is not found in the passage. Often, the answer makes common sense or may be true in the real world. However, on the TOEFL, every correct answer must be found in the passage.
- **Extreme:** These answer choices use wording that is too strong or absolute. These choices usually include words such as *all, always, impossible, must, never,* or *none.* Correct answers on the TOEFL usually do not contain such strong language.
- **Right answer, wrong question:** These choices contain information that is mentioned in the passage; however, the information doesn't answer the question.
- **Verbatim:** Many wrong answers repeat parts of the passage word for word. Unfortunately, the choices use these words in the wrong context or incorrectly. These answers can be especially tempting.

- **Beyond the information:** Choices in this category are based on information in the passage, but they go beyond the given information, meaning that they give more information than the passage provides. For example, if the passage states "some species of chimpanzees make crude tools out of branches," the answer choice may read "many animals can make tools." This answer goes beyond the information by changing "some species of chimpanzees" to "many animals."

When you are preparing for the TOEFL, make sure you review all the questions, even the ones you've gotten right. Read each wrong answer choice, and see if you can figure out what makes it wrong. Becoming familiar with the wrong answers is almost as important as finding the right answers Also, while you are practicing, identify and note *why* certain answers are wrong. Make sure to mark each wrong answer with one of the five categories we discussed in POE: Part II.

CRACKING THE READING SECTION: BASIC APPROACH
When approaching the Reading section of the TOEFL, follow these steps.

> 1. **Actively read the passage,** looking for the purpose, structure, and main idea.
> 2. **Attack the questions** based on question type.
> 3. **Find the answer** to the question in the passage.
> 4. **Use POE** to eliminate bad answers.

Let's look at each of these steps in greater detail.

Step 1: Actively Read the Passage

One of the biggest mistakes you can make on the TOEFL is to attempt to read and understand every single word of the passage. There are many problems with this approach. One is that you simply do not have enough time to read the entire passage and accurately answer all of the questions. A second problem is that there is far more information in the passage than you will ever need to know to answer the questions. The more of the passage that you read, the more likely you are to become confused or distracted. Finally, remember that you get points for answering questions, not reading passages. You want to spend your time answering questions and earning points, not reading.

Here's a passage similar to one you would find on the TOEFL. It should look familiar to you. We used it to introduce you to the look of the test in Part I. Take a few moments to actively read it.

More Available

The Exoskeleton of the Arthropod

There are more arthropods alive on Earth than there are members of any other phylum of animals. Given that not only insects and spiders but also shrimp, crabs, centipedes, and their numerous relatives are arthropods, this fact should not occasion surprise. For all their diversity, arthropods of any type share two defining characteristics: jointed legs (from which the phylum takes its name) and an exoskeleton (the recognizable hard outer shell).

→ Though the shell itself is made of dead tissue like that of human hair and fingernails, it is dotted with sensory cells. These give the arthropod information about its surroundings, much as the nerve endings in human skin do. Also like human skin, the shell protects fragile internal organs from potentially hazardous contact with the environment. It seals in precious moisture that would otherwise evaporate but permits the exchange of gases.

Its primary component is chitin, a natural polymer that contains calcium and is very similar in structure to the cellulose in wood. Chitin and proteins are secreted in the epidermis, the living tissue just below the shell, after which they bond to form a thin sheet. Each new sheet is produced so that its chitin fibers are not parallel with those directly above, which increases their combined strength.

The result is the endocuticle, a mesh of molecules that forms the lowest layer of the shell. The endocuticle is not quite tough enough for daily wear and tear. Over time, however, its molecules continue to lock together. As the endocuticle is pushed upward by the formation of new sheets by the epidermis, it becomes the middle shell layer called the exocuticle. With its

TOEFL Reading

Question 3 of 12

REVIEW | HELP ? | BACK ← | NEXT →

PAUSE TEST | SECTION EXIT

HIDE TIME | 00:08:45

More Available

molecules bonded so tightly, the exocuticle is very durable. There are points on the body where it does not form, since flexibility is needed around joints. This arrangement allows supple movement but provides armor-like protection.

Though strong, the chitin and protein exocuticle itself would provide a poor barrier against moisture loss. Therefore, it must be coated with lipids, which are also secreted by the epidermis. These lipids, mostly fatty acids and waxes, form the third, outermost layer of the shell. They spread over the cuticles to form a waterproof seal even in dry weather. This lipid layer gives many arthropods their distinctive luster.

Combined, the endocuticle, exocuticle, and lipid coating form a shell that provides formidable protection. The external shell has other advantages. One is that, because it has far more surface area than the internal skeleton found in vertebrates, it provides more points at which muscles can be attached. This increased number of muscles permits many arthropods to be stronger and more agile for their body size than birds or mammals. The coloration and markings of the exoskeleton can be beneficial as well. Many species of scorpion, for instance, have cuticles that contain hyaline. The hyaline is excited by ultraviolet radiation, so these scorpions glow blue-green when a black light is flashed on them. Scientists are not sure why scorpions have evolved to fluoresce this way, but the reason may be that their glow attracts insects that they can capture and eat.

Adaptive as the shell is, it leaves arthropods with at least one distinct disadvantage: The cuticle cannot expand to accommodate growth. As the animal increases in size, therefore, it must occasionally molt. The

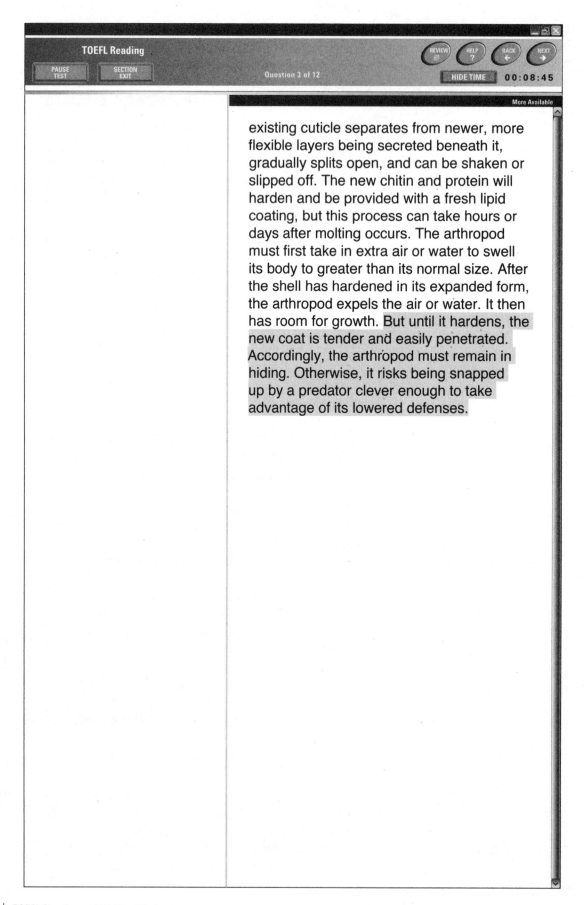

existing cuticle separates from newer, more flexible layers being secreted beneath it, gradually splits open, and can be shaken or slipped off. The new chitin and protein will harden and be provided with a fresh lipid coating, but this process can take hours or days after molting occurs. The arthropod must first take in extra air or water to swell its body to greater than its normal size. After the shell has hardened in its expanded form, the arthropod expels the air or water. It then has room for growth. But until it hardens, the new coat is tender and easily penetrated. Accordingly, the arthropod must remain in hiding. Otherwise, it risks being snapped up by a predator clever enough to take advantage of its lowered defenses.

On the TOEFL, you will see that paragraphs referred to in the questions are marked by a ➔; this will help you quickly locate the paragraphs. You may see black squares ■ in the passage, and some of the words will be shaded in gray, whereas others will be boldfaced. Try not to be distracted by these symbols, words, and phrases—there will be questions about them later, but don't get bogged down by them while you're reading.

Now that you've had a minute to look over this passage, state the main idea. What is the author's purpose, and how is the passage structured?

Main idea: _____

_____

Structure: _____

_____

Purpose: _____

_____

For this passage, the main idea is "arthropods have a tough outer shell that protects them and provides them with other advantages." The structure is fairly typical, with each of the body paragraphs describing some aspect of the shell. The first body paragraph describes the shell itself. The second paragraph tells you the composition of the shell. The third and fourth paragraphs tell you the pros and cons of the shell. The last paragraph presents a disadvantage of the shell. Putting this all together, the author's purpose is "to inform."

Step 2: Attack the Questions

After actively reading the passage, go to the questions. The questions on the TOEFL come in a few different varieties.

Most of the questions are multiple choice, as shown below.

10. Why is an arthropod vulnerable after molting?

(A) It is far from sources of water.
(B) It is more visible to predators.
(C) Its shell is soft.
(D) The loss of energy makes it weak.

Other questions require you to click on part of the passage. These questions look like the following:

15. Look at the four squares [■] in the passage. Where would the following sentence best fit in the passage? Click on the [■] to add the sentence to the passage.

For these questions, you'll have to go back to the passage and click on one of the squares to answer it. Other questions of this variety may ask you to click on a word or phrase.

The final type of question is called a multiple-multiple-choice questions. These questions require you to choose several correct answers.

22. A brief summary of the passage is provided below. Click on the THREE sentences that best complete the summary. Some sentences are not part of the summary because they do not express the main idea. *This question is worth 2 points.*

These questions are followed by several sentences. Use the mouse to drag the sentences you select into the summary box. You can remove one of your choices by clicking on it again.

In general, the multiple-choice questions are the easiest. You should do them on your first pass. The summary questions—the multiple-multiple-choice ones—take the longest, so save them for last. (They usually turn up at the end anyway.) The passage-based questions fall somewhere in between these two.

Question Types

The questions on the Reading section of the TOEFL can be grouped into several different categories. Each question requires its own strategy, but remember that for each question, the answer is somewhere in the passage. Also, some questions are much more common than others, so you may not see all of the following types when you take the TOEFL.

The question types on the TOEFL are as follows:

1. **Vocabulary in context:** These are some of the most common questions on the TOEFL. You may be asked the meaning of a word or phrase. These questions are some of the easiest, so do them on your first pass.

2. **Reference:** These questions usually ask you what noun a pronoun connects to, though sometimes they may ask you about a noun, adverb, or adjective. Because these questions also direct you to a certain point in the passage, do these on your first pass.

3. **Lead words:** Some questions will refer to a word highlighted in gray in the passage. Other questions may ask about a specific word or phrase, even if there is nothing highlighted in the passage. Also do these on your first pass.

4. **Detail:** Often the easiest type of question, detail questions ask about specific facts from the passage. Again, get these questions done on your first pass.

5. **Paraphrase:** Paraphrase questions ask you to find the answer choice that means the same as a bolded sentence in the passage.

6. **Definition:** This type of question asks you to find the part of the passage that defines a certain word or phrase.

7. **Before/after:** These questions are rare. They ask you what kind of paragraph would likely precede or follow the passage.

8. **Sentence insertion:** For this type of question, you'll see four black squares (■) placed throughout the passage. Your job is to figure out in which of these spots a new sentence would best fit.

9. **EXCEPT/NOT/LEAST:** These questions can be some of the most difficult on the test so save them for the second pass. For these, you are looking for the answer that is *not* supported by the passage. EXCEPT/NOT/LEAST questions also tend to take longer to answer than most multiple-choice questions.

10. **Inference:** This popular question type can be one of the trickiest types; therefore, you'll want to save these questions for the second pass. Inference questions ask you to find the statement that is implied or suggested by the passage. Remember, the TOEFL uses a narrow interpretation of *inference*, and correct responses to these questions *must be true* based on the information provided in the passage.

11. **Summary:** Typically worth two points, these questions ask you to find main points and ideas from the passage. Because they require some knowledge of the passage, do them on your second pass after you have had a chance to become familiar with the material.

Familiarize yourself with this list. As you'll see, being able to recognize the question types will aid you in both your approach to finding the answer and your POE strategy.

Step 3: Find the Answer in the Passage and Use POE

As we've stated before—and it cannot be emphasized enough—the correct answer to each question is *always* found in the passage. The trick on the TOEFL is, of course, finding that answer in an efficient manner. Fortunately, each question provides a clue, or hint, as to where we need to look for our answer.

Here is our general system for dealing with questions on the TOEFL.

1. **Read and rephrase the question.** You'll notice that many questions on the TOEFL are not written in a straightforward manner. Before you head back to the passage to find the answer, make sure you understand what the question is asking you to find.

2. **Go back to the passage and find the answer.** The question will direct you to the appropriate part of the passage. Go back to the passage and read enough lines (about six) to get the context of the text. Essentially, you are looking for a "window" in the passge where the answer will be. Never answer a question from memory alone because you're more likely to fall for a trap answer.

3. **Answer in your own words first.** This is the most important step of all. After returning to the passage and reading the appropriate part of it, you should be able to answer the question in your own words. If you can't, you may be reading the wrong part of the passage or you may need to read more lines. If you are having a hard time doing this in the beginning don't worry. Keep practicing it!

4. **Use POE.** Once you have an idea of the type of answer for which you're looking, return to the question and use POE.

Make sure to practice this system on each question until it becomes automatic. The best way to approach the TOEFL is to have a clear, consistent plan of attack. The next chapter contains practice reading drills. The answers can be found in Chapter 6.

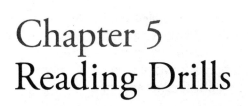

Chapter 5
Reading Drills

Reading Drill #1

Commedia Dell'arte

Flourishing in Italy from the sixteenth to the eighteenth centuries, *commedia dell'arte* is a distinctive style of comedy that employed masked characters. The name of the form sometimes confuses modern readers. In fact, even some published reference works incorrectly state that the correct English translation is "comedy of artists." A better rendering is something like "drama of artisans." In the Italian spoken when *commedia dell'arte* was current, *commedia* did not refer exclusively to comic theater, and *arte* was used in connection with craftsmen and skilled workers such as leatherworkers and carpenters.

Commedia dell'arte, unlike the literary comedy of the Renaissance, did not require written scripts. Rather, it was a theater of improvisation. It began with street performers. They put on masks and used overdone gestures to represent characters and get laughs. Because it began among performers who did acrobatics and juggling, the developing form retained an emphasis on physical movement.

Instead of memorizing a performance line for line and gesture for gesture, actors combined variable plotlines with stock characters. These characters exaggerated the stereotypes of doctors, merchants, lawyers and other unpopular occupations present in Italian society at the time. The humor was very broad—subtlety was a hallmark of many artistic achievements of the period, but not the *commedia dell'arte*. The actors poked fun at the different regions of Italy by speaking in overdone local accents.

To perfect their portrayals of these standard characters, actors had to develop distinctive skills. The plays they performed were improvised, but actors still needed a basic set of routine scenes and situations that could be altered in unexpected ways from one performance to another. It was common for an **actor** in the *commedia dell'arte* to choose a **type** of **role** and **specialize** in it for life. Most actors kept notebooks, *zibaldone*, in which they noted down monologues, dialogues, and tag lines that their characters regularly rehearsed with. Additionally, the immobile masks most characters wore prevented them from using facial expressions to convey emotions. To accustom themselves to conveying mood exclusively through gesture and tone of voice, new actors practiced a variety of characters with a neutral mask. This was a wooden mask, without the markings for any specific character, used exclusively to remind an actor not to use his face to emote during rehearsals.

The unpredictable nature of *commedia dell'arte* helped account for its extraordinary popularity and influence. But it did not help the form to develop over time. What had been a fresh and interesting method of improvisation at the end of the Renaissance turned stale by the end of the eighteenth century. Many of the characters, having been standardized for centuries, were no longer relevant to a changing Italy, in which a conservative revolution was occurring both in society and in the theater. The popularity of *commedia dell'arte* decreased as it alienated the emerging middle-class audience. Audiences had tired of jokes in questionable taste, and they faulted the plotlines for not flowing believably and lacking a clear message. The use of improvisation had started in the Renaissance as a break from traditional passion plays, with their sober, predetermined storylines. As *commedia dell'arte* progressively became an institutionalized form of theater, improvisation itself began to seem old-fashioned.

As a result, the *commedia dell'arte* was transformed. It evolved from presenting improvised performances of stereotyped characters toward following a script. The resulting performances both relied less on character types and expressed a clear moral lesson. Despite its ultimate decline, however, its influence on European drama can be easily detected: French pantomime and the English harlequinade took character types directly from the *commedia dell'arte*. The classic French playwright Molière created some of his most famous characters from the raw materials of villains of the *commedia dell'arte*. Even today, many modern stage movements and settings can be traced back to it.

1. How did *commedia dell'arte* differ from Renaissance comedy?

   (A) Roles in Renaissance comedy included doctors and lawyers.
   (B) *Commedia dell'arte* was performed outdoors.
   (C) Renaissance comedy was scripted.
   (D) The actors of Renaissance comedy weren't paid.

2. The word broad in the passage is closest in meaning to

   (A) exciting
   (B) timeless
   (C) comic
   (D) exaggerated

3. Underline the word or phrase in bold text that it refers to.

4. Actors in the *commedia dell'arte* made fun of different regions through their

   (A) occupations
   (B) costumes
   (C) speech patterns
   (D) conservatism

5. The author implies that *zibaldone*

   (A) were read aloud during performances
   (B) helped the performers develop their characters
   (C) relaxed the audience members
   (D) were valued by Renaissance actors

6. It may be inferred from paragraph 4 that which of the following made *commedia dell'arte* unpredictable?

   (A) Its fluctuations in popularity
   (B) The various Italian accents used by actors
   (C) The use of actors from different regions
   (D) Improvised combinations of stock scenes

7. The word stale in the passage is closest in meaning to

   (A) popular
   (B) historical
   (C) boring
   (D) unclear

8. The word progressively in the passage is closest in meaning to

   (A) gradually
   (B) purposefully
   (C) suddenly
   (D) unnoticeably

9. Each of the following is a reason the *commedia dell'arte* decreased in popularity EXCEPT

   (A) people became more conservative
   (B) plot lines were too simple
   (C) the audience tired of vulgar comedy
   (D) improvisation no longer seemed interesting

10. According to the passage, what was a result of the transformation of *commedia dell'arte*?

   (A) The performances were shorter.
   (B) Audience members felt it lacked humor.
   (C) Plots had a more obvious message.
   (D) Theatergoers became less conservative.

11. Underline the sentence in paragraph 5 in which the author describes specific ways that theatergoers became more conservative.

12. The word detected in the passage is closest in meaning to

    (A) seen
    (B) performed
    (C) translated
    (D) increased

13. Directions: An introductory sentence for a brief summary of the passage is provided below. Complete the summary by selecting the THREE answer choices that express the most important ideas in the passage. Some sentences do not belong in the summary because they express ideas that are not presented in the passage or are minor details in the passage. This question is worth 2 points.

    The *commedia dell'arte* was a form of Italian theater that rose and fell in popularity between the sixteenth and eighteenth centuries.

    -
    -
    -

Answer Choices

Actors used exaggerated gestures, accents, and masks to give comic performances of stock characters.	Similar kinds of improvised comic theater were developing in other European countries during the same period.
"Comedy of artists" is not the best translation of *commedia dell'arte*.	The *commedia dell'arte*'s origin in street theater produced its emphasis on improvised performances.
Commedia dell'arte was forced to evolve when its vulgarity and lack of clear storylines lost favor with audiences.	An unmarked mask was used to help actors practice their characters.

Reading Drill #2

Candles in Colonial America

The lack of artificial sources of light meant that most colonial Americans had to begin and end their day's activities with the sun. Houses, shops, and workrooms were usually oriented so their long sides faced east and west. This allowed the walls of the building with the largest surface areas to be devoted to windows that captured the strongest light as the sun traversed the sky. In winter, the duration in which daylight was strong decreased, and what light there was tended to be pale. Craftspersons usually saw their productivity fall accordingly.

Those who needed light for reading or working by night generally relied on candles which at that time were of generally inferior quality. The wick of a modern candle is designed to burn down as the wax does, so a candle can be left burning for long periods. The wicks of colonial candles, however, burned more slowly than the wax they were drawing up. This meant that candles had to be frequently "snuffed," that is, the **wick** cut off so that it didn't droop over as the wax burned out from under it. A special tool for snipping the wick was used, and care had to be taken to cut enough of the wick away without putting out the flame.

The wax itself was also a problem. Most new colonists would likely have preferred candles of beeswax, which burned smoothly, slowly and cleanly and produced a pleasing fragrance. Unfortunately, beeswax for candles was too dear for most households to afford for daily use in lighting. The most common candle type, in North America as in Europe, was made of tallow, the fat that melted from cow's or sheep's meat during roasting. A pan would be put in underneath the cooking meat to catch the tallow as it ran out. When the pan was set aside, the collected **tallow** congealed as it cooled. Since juices and small pieces of meat were invariably mixed in, it had to be purified before use. When the women of a household had reserved enough tallow from a series of meals, they melted it again in large **kettles**. To create candles, they repeatedly dipped wicks of cotton or linen into the tallow, allowing each new layer to cool and harden before the next dipping. This laborious process produced tapers, a type of tall, narrow candle with a thick base.

Though tallow candles were the least costly night lighting available to the average family, they were difficult to use. On summer days, high temperatures could soften stored candles until the fat and wick separated, making them unusable. (The tallow could, however, be saved, melted again, and made into more candles when the weather cooperated.) They were also inconvenient. A burning tallow candle emitted a strong, unpleasant odor, and it produced almost as much smoke as light. Furthermore, tallow burned unevenly: candles often hissed, popped, and spluttered.

■An alternative material for candles, which shared many of the desirable properties of beeswax, was discovered in the bayberry, a flowering plant native to the Eastern Seaboard. The plant had tough, nut-like fruits that could be harvested like other berries in season. Colonial women found that by boiling the fruits, they could extract their waxy **coating**. The yield in finished candles was small, like that of beeswax (even if bayberry wax was as easy to process as tallow). ■Fifteen pounds of bayberries were required to produce just one pound of wax, so bayberry wax was more expensive than tallow. But there were compensations for people used to depending on fickle and uncooperative tallow candles. Candles made from bayberry wax burned consistently and brightly, with little smoke. Their fragrance, like that of the berries themselves, was pleasant. ■ Records from the period indicate that bayberry candles eventually nearly equaled tallow candles in popularity. ■ Even so, it was not until the next century that further innovations made the true mass production of inexpensive, high-quality wax candles possible.

1. The word oriented in the passage is closest in meaning to

   (A) worked in
   (B) laid out
   (C) brightened
   (D) heated

2. The word duration in the passage is closest in meaning to

   (A) period
   (B) region
   (C) angle
   (D) necessity

3. The word dear in the passage is closest in meaning to

   (A) attractive
   (B) rare
   (C) expensive
   (D) thick

4. The word they in the passage refers to

   (A) tall candles
   (B) large kettles
   (C) a series of meals
   (D) the women of a household

5. Which of the following is an advantage of tallow candles?

   (A) Low cost
   (B) Even burning
   (C) Pleasant fragrance
   (D) Bright light

6. The word them in the passage refers to

   (A) high temperatures
   (B) summer days
   (C) most families
   (D) stored candles

7. Underline the term in **bold** text that is defined in the passage.

8. Why were bayberry candles expensive for the colonists?

   (A) The berries were rare and hard to find.
   (B) Extracting the wax required time and effort.
   (C) Each berry produced little wax.
   (D) The fragrance made the candles a luxury.

9. Why does the author mention records from the colonial period in paragraph 5?

   (A) Records list the advantages of bayberry over tallow.
   (B) Records show when colonists first made tallow candles.
   (C) Records show bayberry candles were commonly used.
   (D) There are no records of the first candles mass-produced in the colonies.

10. Underline the square where the following sentence would best fit if added to the passage.

    These advantages seem to have made bayberry candles worth the extra cost for colonists.

11. Paragraph 5 mainly discusses

    (A) the process of extracting wax from bayberries
    (B) the first mass production of bayberry candles
    (C) why the bayberry was suited to candle making
    (D) the source of the bayberry's fragrance

12. The word yield in the passage refers to

    (A)   how many candles could be produced
    (B)   how much light bayberry candles emitted
    (C)   how convenient bayberry candles were to use
    (D)   how long it took to remove the waxy coating from bayberries

13. Directions: An introductory sentence for a brief summary of the passage is provided below. Complete the summary by selecting the THREE answer choices that express the most important ideas in the passage. Some sentences do not belong in the summary because they express ideas that are not presented in the passage or are minor details in the passage. This question is worth 2 points.

The candles colonists relied on to provide artificial light presented many difficulties.

-
-
-

Answer Choices	
The most common candles were made of tallow, an animal fat that gave poor light.	Candle makers were busy and often saw their productivity fall in winter.
Candles made of bayberry wax had many advantages that made them popular despite their expense.	Beeswax was a material that produced candles with a pleasant fragrance.
It took the colonists many years before they discovered how to extract wax from bayberries.	Candle wicks burned slowly and needed constant attention.

Reading Drill #3

The Triune Brain Hypothesis

The structure of the human brain is still incompletely understood. That the brain has distinct regions at which different activities are centered is well accepted, although it is now known that few functions are performed exclusively by a single section of the brain. This adaptation prevents crucial functions from being lost if a given region of the brain is injured. Even so, most activities are centered in identifiable areas of a normal, healthy brain. When scientists measure brain function while experimental subjects are speaking, reading, or writing, certain parts of the brain tend to show more electrical activity than others.

Still, how the brain's regions relate to one another is still a matter of dispute and will likely remain so for some time, given the extraordinary complexity of their interactions. One theory, called the "triune brain hypothesis," holds that what we think of as our single brain is actually three distinct bodies. The functions of these bodies reflect our different ancestral relationships to reptiles, early mammals, and later mammals. This hypothesis was developed by researcher Paul MacLean, who refers to each body as a separate brain.

The first brain is the R-complex, so called because we inherited it from our reptile ancestors. Within this complex are the nerves that control self-defense and preservation of the species. By experimenting with the **R-complex** in **animals** such as squirrel monkeys and turkeys, **MacLean** has shown that it contains the **programs** responsible for hunting, homing, mating, establishing territory, and fighting. These are basic functions for survival that were necessary from the time even the most rudimentary advances in intelligence were taking place in the animal kingdom. In structural terms, the R-complex is an expansion of the upper brainstem, where the brain meets the spinal cord.

The second brain is the limbic system, which controls impulses more complex than self-preservation. The limbic system is not present in reptiles; it developed in early mammals. It's functions are of a higher order than those of the R-complex: after destruction of part of the limbic system, young mammals stop playing, and parents nurture their young less. That is, sophisticated social interactions cease. MacLean describes this as a "reptilian condition," as if mammals without functioning limbic systems had turned back into their reptile ancestors.

What distinguishes higher mammals from earlier mammals is the cortex. ■This is the third brain according to the triune brain hypothesis, and it is most highly developed in humans. The cortex seems to control the memorization and problem-solving needed to aid the two older bodies in the struggle for survival. MacLean considers the cortex like a computer that can look into the future and anticipate the consequences of actions. ■This is, of course, the most advanced kind of intelligence—the ability to think about things that are not actually happening or things that are not actually present at the time. The cortex is thus the source of many behaviors we associate with primates. ■

■Scientists studying the cortex have found that it has constituent parts of its own. The prefrontal areas of the cortex are the most highly developed. According to triune brain theory, the development of these parts of the cortex was the most auspicious turn of events in the history of biology. They are the site of self-awareness in the brain, the part that coordinates the R-complex, the limbic system, and the rest of the cortex to take complex actions for survival. According to MacLean's model, it is the prefrontal region of the cortex that is able to anticipate and fulfill the needs of others as well as the self and one's immediate kin group. In MacLean's words, "It is this new development that makes possible the insight required to plan for the needs of others as well as the self and to use our knowledge to alleviate suffering everywhere."

1. What is the passage mainly about?

   (A) the use of computers to study the brain
   (B) similarities in reptile and mammal brains
   (C) the discovery of the cortex in the human brain
   (D) an interpretation of how parts of the human brain work

2. Select the answer choice below that is closest in meaning to the word holds.

   (A) has no opinion about
   (B) considers true
   (C) grasps ideas quickly
   (D) talks too much

3. Underline the word in the bold text in paragraph 3 that it refers to.

4. The author implies that the limbic system

   (A) contains programs for hunting
   (B) is a site of our sense of play
   (C) helps us look into the future
   (D) destroys the R-complex

5. It can be inferred from the passage that the cortex

   (A) controls emotional behavior
   (B) receives symbols from the R-complex
   (C) is a recent development in the history of the brain
   (D) controls self-preservation

6. According to the passage, which of the following is true of the prefrontal areas of the human cortex?

   (A) They are the most highly developed parts of the cortex.
   (B) They are similar to comparable areas in other mammals.
   (C) They do not communicate with the limbic system.
   (D) They are the site of self-preservation instinct.

7. Underline the sentence in paragraph 5 in which MacLean uses an analogy to describe how part of the brain functions.

8. Select the following answer choice that is closest in meaning to turn of events.

    (A) complexity
    (B) necessity
    (C) experiment
    (D) change

9. Select the answer choice below that is most similar in meaning to alleviate.

    (A) lessen
    (B) include
    (C) balance
    (D) eliminate

10. Underline the square where the following sentence would best fit if added to the passage.

    The cerebral cortex furnishes us with the capabilities that make such planning possible: language, reason, and understanding symbols.

11. According to the passage, which of the following is an animal studied by MacLean?

    (A) dog
    (B) turkey
    (C) lizard
    (D) rat

12. Which of the sentences below best expresses the essential information in the highlighted sentence in the passage? *Incorrect* choices change the meaning in important ways or leave out essential information.

    (A) In general, any given function can be performed by several regions of the brain, but tends to be concentrated in one special area.
    (B) Scientists are not sure whether most functions are performed by one area of the brain exclusively.
    (C) Each single section of the brain can perform many functions.
    (D) Scientists have researched many brain functions, but they have only discovered a few that are centered in particular regions.

13. Directions: An introductory sentence for a brief summary of the passage is provided below. Complete the summary by selecting the THREE answer choices that express the most important ideas in the passage. Some sentences do not belong in the summary because they express ideas that are not presented in the passage or are minor details in the passage. This question is worth 2 points.

Researcher Paul McLean has developed a theory of the human brain called the triune brain hypothesis.

-
-
-

Answer Choices	
McLean works with several types of animals to find similarities between their brains and ours.	Scientists study brain function by measuring electrical activity while subjects speak, read, and write.
The cortex is the part of the brain humans share with higher mammals, their closest modern-day relatives.	The R-complex and the limbic system are parts of the brain inherited from ancient ancestors.
McLean's theory is highly controversial, though no specific component of it has been disproved.	The prefrontal areas of the cortex may be the site of the self-awareness and generosity we think of as characteristically human.

Reading Drill #4

Thomas Eakins's Painting

The value placed on realism in art has varied by time and place. Rather than accurately depicting an object as the human eye would see it, artists have sometimes emphasized the effects of light, or idealized color, and form. These techniques have been intended to express various artistic truths that cannot be conveyed through simple physical realism.

But a select few artists have managed to combine exacting surface realism with depth of expressiveness. One such example is Philadelphia native Thomas Eakins (1844–1916), frequently considered the greatest American painter. Eakins trained from the very beginning of his career to synthesize realism with inspiration. He studied at the Pennsylvania Academy of the Fine Arts, and for a few years in Europe. But he also enrolled in an anatomy course at the Thomas Jefferson Medical College. **The school's dissecting rooms were not normal places for young artists to visit, but Eakins insisted that he wanted to know from the inside how the human body worked.** He learned how the skeleton was fitted together, and he learned how flesh and skin were layered over it. Therefore, when he used a live model for sketching or painting, his eye perceived more than the model's outward appearance. He knew which movements of bone and muscle were involved in sitting, standing, and forming various facial expressions.

Eakins was not afraid to give his medical knowledge direct expression in his art. **When he wanted to attract attention with a major picture, he painted a surgical operation:** *The Gross Clinic.* The **surgery** depicted was a routine **procedure**, but the **painting** was a departure from artistic **convention**, and it caused a great deal of controversy when completed. It was Eakins's matter-of-fact inclusion of blood on the hands of the surgeon that was considered scandalous. **Paintings from battles of the Civil War had often portrayed the wounded as bleeding, but Eakins's contemporaries in polite Philadelphian society believed blood had no place in art that depicted daily life.** *The Gross Clinic* was refused exhibition. Eakins finally sold the large canvas, today considered a masterpiece, for a very small sum to a medical school.

Most paintings by Eakins used his knowledge of anatomy less directly than *The Gross Clinic.* As his career progressed, he painted many pictures of athletes in motion: rowers, swimmers, and hunters. **The moments he chose to depict were frequently those at which muscles were most contracted or extended, in order to capture peaks of tension.** His knowledge of anatomy helped him to render these extremes of activity very effectively. In addition, the outdoor setting provided Eakins with the opportunity to work with variations of perspective, light, and shadow. He also felt, unlike many artists of the time, that the emerging medium of photography was of great use in learning about the human form in motion.

During his later years, Eakins concentrated on portraits, mostly of his friends and family. In these paintings, the bone and muscle structures beneath the skin were suggested with subtle variations of paint color and texture. Eakins was sometimes criticized for painting with such precise realism that he made people look more old and tired than they actually were. This was in part a by-product of Eakins's painstaking technique. He required his models to sit for a long time, which made it difficult for them to retain their formal posture. As they relaxed, they unconsciously revealed more of their inner thoughts. Eakins captured those thoughts on canvas. In his portraits, viewers can see fear, doubt, and anxiety. But Eakins's technique also lent his subjects an air of thoughtfulness. By refusing to idealize them, he showed them to be people with complex personalities. These portraits were at the opposite extreme from the creations of fashionable painters of the day.

The artistic success of these paintings lies in how they combine Eakins's artistic and medical training. Understanding bone and muscle structure allowed him to create two-dimensional paintings in which people seem to exist with depth, weight, and emotion. He achieved this so successfully that few other painters can rival him. Most interestingly, he achieved these high points of realism in art while anti-naturalistic movements in Modern art were gaining ascendancy.

1. Which of the following is the main point the passage makes about Thomas Eakins?

    (A) He developed a special kind of realism.
    (B) He tended to paint pictures of unhappy people.
    (C) He liked to paint realistic scenes that shocked people.
    (D) His art was more popular in France than in America.

2. Underline the word or phrase in bold text that it refers to.

3. The passage implies that Eakins differed from other artists in which of the following ways?

    (A) He painted large canvases.
    (B) He studied art in France rather than at home.
    (C) He painted blood in battle scenes.
    (D) He formally studied anatomy.

4. What can be inferred about fashionable painters in Eakins's time?

    (A) They studied anatomy to help them paint realistically.
    (B) They painted pictures of their friends.
    (C) They did not emphasize thoughtfulness in their portraits.
    (D) They never painted battle paintings.

5. Paragraph 4 implies that Eakins used which of the following to help him paint expressively?

    (A) Bone and muscle structure
    (B) Advice from other painters
    (C) Cubism
    (D) Other examples of good realistic painting

6. In calling *The Gross Clinic* a major picture, the author means that it was a

    (A) portrait of a person
    (B) painting that attracted attention
    (C) popular painting
    (D) very big painting

7. Which of the following answer choices is closest in meaning to routine?

    (A) Obedient
    (B) Ordinary
    (C) Unknown
    (D) Innovative

8. Select the answer choice to which contemporaries in the passage refers.

    (A) Surgeons
    (B) Paris art students
    (C) Americans in the late nineteenth century
    (D) Rival painters

9. The passage would probably continue with a discussion of

    (A) other realistic artists
    (B) Modern art that was not naturalistic
    (C) Eakins's final paintings
    (D) other artists who studied medicine

10. Underline the sentence in **bold** text that describes what Eakins was attempting in his paintings of athletes. (Scroll the passage to see all of the answer choices.)

11. In paragraph 3, why does the author mention that *The Gross Clinic* was sold for a very small sum to a medical school?

    (A) To contrast the painting with his high-priced potraits
    (B) To show that blood was considered unacceptable in paintings
    (C) To emphasize that the painting was undervalued as a work of art
    (D) To demonstrate the extent to which the painting attracted attention

12. According to the passage, Eakins achieved the famous effects in his portrait paintings by doing all of the following EXCEPT

(A) frequently painting surgeons at work
(B) requiring models to sit for a long time
(C) depicting his subjects without idealizing them
(D) suggesting the bones and muscles under the skin

13. Directions: An introductory sentence for a brief summary of the passage is provided below. Complete the summary by selecting the THREE answer choices that express the most important ideas in the passage. Some sentences do not belong in the summary because they express ideas that are not presented in the passage or are minor details in the passage. This question is worth 2 points.

Thomas Eakins developed a unique style of painting based on his training and approach to his subjects.

-
-
-

Answer Choices	
He painted very realistically, without making people's features look artificially happy.	One of Eakins's most famous paintings was initially refused exhibition.
He took photographs in addition to painting.	He used paint effects to suggest underlying body structures.
He studied anatomy as well as taking art training.	He spent most of his life painting scenes from his native Philadelphia.

Reading Drill #5

Flax Fibers

Prehistoric humans learned to make linen yarn from flax before they learned to make yarn from the wool of sheep. It was a breakthrough that took quite a bit of time to work up to; however, the flax plant does not appear to the untrained eye to be a promising source of yarn soft enough to use in textile production. The fibers of the flax plant are hidden within its stem. **Harvesting** them requires peeling the outer layer of the stem away and, in turn, pulling the fibers themselves away from the plant's brittle, woody pith.

But the difficulties with obtaining usable flax began long before the fibers were freed from the hard tissue surrounding them. In order to produce fibers that are long enough to spin into yarn, farmers must cultivate flax plants in "close stands," clustering them tightly. This method assures that the stems do not have room to form branches as the plants grow. Once suitably long, straight stalks have been successfully grown, they are harvested and processed. The raw fibers are too inflexible to use in textiles, and they stick to other parts of the plant. So before removal from the stems they must be softened. The process generally used is natural and has been known since ancient times. Flax farmers let the stems sit in a warm, moist environment to allow fermenting bacteria to digest them partially. This process is called **retting**. **Bleaching** is usually done chemically in modern production facilities, though a combination of simple chemicals and sunlight is the method human societies first used.

Growing, harvesting, and processing flax plants is very complex, but many cultures through history have considered them worth the trouble. The linen thread spun from the fibers is very versatile. Excavations of Egyptian tombs have recovered fragments of linen cloth that date back to 1500 BCE. The fine tunics of royalty, aristocrats, and priests in paintings are also of linen, which is easy to pleat into the neat patterns the Egyptians preferred. Indeed, the best Egyptian linen was so finely woven that when it was found on mummies discovered in the twentieth century, it was in a state of almost perfect preservation. This indicates that the microorganisms that cause decay of most organic materials tend not to attack flax fibers, giving justification to the ancient association of linen with cleanliness and purity. Later, the Roman Empire consumed a great deal of linen and introduced flax seeds into Northern Europe to provide another source of fibers. Huguenots from what is now France brought flax seed and cultivation methods to Ireland, which has since gone on to produce some of the world's finest linens. Items made of Irish linen are almost always prominently labeled, since they still have a worldwide reputation and command a high price.

■ Linen fibers adapted readily to being incorporated into garments, sailcloth, writing paper, and insulation. ■ Mechanical looms developed in the sixteenth century sped the weaving of cotton, but they pulled yarns too roughly to be used with delicate linen. **Creasing repeatedly** along the same line will also eventually cause **cracks** to appear in **linen**. Still, though **flax fibers** are less flexible than **cotton fibers**, they are longer and stronger overall. Since finely woven linen is so smooth and lustrous, it is one of the most valuable textiles. ■ Like cotton, linen conducts heat and, therefore, is ideal for being made into garments that feel cool even in hot and humid weather. ■ Because of this impressive combination of qualities, engineers continued to look for ways to adjust mechanical looms to make them more suited to processing flax. Today, mass production of linen uses machines that are sensitive enough to pull the fibers taut without straining them.

1. What does the passage mainly discuss?

    (A) How prehistoric humans learned to make fabric
    (B) Where flax is easiest to grow and harvest
    (C) How flax is obtained and used
    (D) Which developments in loom design made weaving easier

2. The word brittle in the passage is closest in meaning to

    (A) lasting
    (B) outer
    (C) stiff
    (D) hidden

3. The purpose of paragraph 3 is to

    (A) show that linen was widely used in history
    (B) argue that techniques for processing flax were more advanced in Egypt
         than in Rome
    (C) show that linen has historically been too expensive for most people to
         buy
    (D) discuss differences in quality among Egyptian, Roman, and Irish linens

4. The word clustering in the passage is closest in meaning to

    (A) digging
    (B) binding
    (C) grouping
    (D) harvesting

5. What problem does planting flax in "close stands" solve?

    (A) Fibers that are too brittle to use
    (B) Fibers that are too short to use
    (C) A low number of flax plants per field
    (D) The slow growth of flax plants

6. A warm, moist environment is used in processing flax fibers in order to

    (A) make them strong enough to use on power looms
    (B) use warm water to clean them
    (C) separate them from the pith of the flax stem
    (D) break them down until they are softer

7. Select the following answer choice to which them refers.

    (A)   fibers
    (B)   textiles
    (C)   farmers
    (D)   bacteria

8. According to the passage, the ancient Egyptian linen that still exists demonstrates that

    (A)   most ancient societies wove linen fibers into detailed patterns
    (B)   linen is durable and resists decay
    (C)   the Romans learned to make pleated linen from the Egyptians
    (D)   linen weaving techniques took thousands of years to develop

9. Underline the **bold-faced word** or **phrase** in the passage to which they refers.

10. According to the passage, each of the following is a characteristic of high-quality linen fibers EXCEPT

    (A)   smoothness
    (B)   flexibility
    (C)   luster
    (D)   coolness

11. Underline the phrase in **bold text** that represents an action that can damage linen fabric. (Scroll the passage to see all of the answer choices.)

12. Underline the square where the following sentence would best fit if added to the passage.

> **Nevertheless, they did not always adapt to advances in the designs of looms themselves.**

13. Directions: An introductory sentence for a brief summary of the passage is provided below. Complete the summary by selecting the THREE answer choices that express the most important ideas in the passage. Some sentences do not belong in the summary because they express ideas that are not presented in the passage or are minor details in the passage. This question is worth 2 points.

Linen cloth made from flax fibers requires effort to produce but has many advantages.

-
-
-

Answer Choices	
As linen has become more popular, Ireland is competing with other sources of linen for customers.	The Egyptians associated linen with royalty and the priesthood.
When properly processed, linen fibers are strong and conduct heat well.	The fibers are not visible when the flax plant is viewed from the outside.
Flax plants must be specially cultivated and softened before the fibers can be removed and processed for use.	More sensitive machines used in processing have made it easier to mass-produce linen for modern consumers.

Reading Drill #6

Defenses of Moths

In biological terms, moths and butterflies are members of the same order, *Lepidoptera*. But while butterflies have a more eminent place in the popular imagination, moths are greater in total numbers and in number of species. Moth species vary greatly: in size, their wingspans vary from one inch to nearly a foot, and moths are found in nearly every climate. Some pollinate plants, others destroy crops, and a few even suck blood from unlucky animals. A number of species are diurnal, but most hunt, mate and migrate at night.

Like many other insects, moths have developed an array of strategies to avoid being eaten by predators. Methods moths use for survival are often fascinating and highly developed. One is camouflage, in which a moth's shape and coloring imitate either a stick or a leaf to blend in with the environment. The moth's disguise only needs to be passable enough to fool forest animals, whose vision generally has low resolution power; however, many actually look amazingly realistic even close up.

Camouflage is not the only kind of mimicry available to moths. Predators tend to avoid poisonous insects, or those that can somehow fight back effectively, such as killer wasps and bees. A moth that has developed to look like one of these inedible insects, however, can confuse and keep away predators even though it does not pose the same dangers. And some moths with protective appearances don't look like either a leaf or a dangerous insect. Rather, their wings have large, eye-shaped markings that make them look threatening. These markings are especially helpful because, again, most moths can make few real threats toward predators and therefore cannot defend themselves easily against attack. In fact, the counterattacks that moths are actually capable of making are usually chemical. One species spits formic acid into its enemy's eyes, blinding and stinging it long enough to escape. The tiger moth's technique is less menacing but just as effective: it secretes a fluid with such a highly offensive odor that predators are quickly turned away.

Of course, adult moths don't always need defensive chemicals or markings, because they can frequently fly away from attackers. However, even at earlier, less mobile phases of the life cycle, moths have a diverse set of survival techniques. In the larval stage, the moth is a caterpillar, wingless but long with many legs. As long as it buys enough time to crawl away, even a temporary diversion will usually give it time to escape. The monkey moth caterpillar has long tips on its legs that are simply extensions of its exoskeleton (hard outer covering). If it gets into trouble, the caterpillar thrusts these extensions toward a predator. The caterpillar is unharmed if a predator breaks off these extensions, which regrow later.

An even more dangerous phase is the pupal phase, when the caterpillar has wrapped itself in a cocoon for the final transformation into a winged adult and thus cannot crawl away from a hungry attacker. At this phase, a developing moth is least mobile and most vulnerable to attack. Pupated moths usually rely on caterpillars and adult members of their colony for protection. The **caterpillars** of the Eastern tent moth weave a communal silk **tent** in which **hundreds or thousands** can go into the pupal phase. If threatened, they have a **shared** strategy for frightening predators: they thrash about, thus shaking the tent. This makes the mass of tiny caterpillars and pupae look like a single large organism, which encourages predators to look for easier prey. If this strategy fails, the Eastern tent caterpillars emit a mixture of noxious chemicals. Other types of moths lack such spectacular defenses, but they still have ways to keep their pupae from being easy targets. In some species, pupae are harbored out of sight under the surface of the soil or water, with plants or twigs used for additional coverage.

1. Which aspect of moths does the passage mainly discuss?

    (A) rapid evolution
    (B) methods of finding food
    (C) differences from butterflies
    (D) survival strategies

2. The word eminent in the passage is closest in meaning to

    (A) ancient
    (B) changing
    (C) major
    (D) beautiful

3. It can be inferred from the passage that a minority of moths

    (A) are active during the day
    (B) benefit from extreme living conditions
    (C) are smaller than butterflies
    (D) do not use camouflage to avoid predators

4. The phrase blend in with the environment implies that some moths are able to

    (A) fight back against predators
    (B) avoid being seen
    (C) hide under twigs and leaves
    (D) find new habitats

5. Underline the **word** or **phrase in bold text** in the passage that is closest in meaning to communal.

6. What kind of adaptation makes a moth appear more threatening?

    (A) Camouflage
    (B) Eye-like markings
    (C) Mimicking a leaf or twig
    (D) Removable leg extensions

7. Select the following answer choice that is closest in meaning to the word pose.

   (A) endure
   (B) present
   (C) collect
   (D) feed

8. How do Eastern tent moths frighten predators?

   (A) Blending in with the silk of their tent
   (B) Making the tent move
   (C) Weaving their tent underwater
   (D) Attacking predators in large groups

9. The word harbored in the passage is closest in meaning to

   (A) lifted
   (B) moved
   (C) built
   (D) hidden

10. According to the passage, moths in the pupal stage are vulnerable to attack because

   (A) there are few places to hide them
   (B) their coloring makes them visible
   (C) they cannot move easily
   (D) there is little food available

11. The passage mentions which of the following as a survival strategy of moths at BOTH adult and pupal phases?

   (A) Mimicking leaves
   (B) Releasing chemicals
   (C) Leg extensions
   (D) Living underground

12. Which of the sentences below best expresses the essential information in the highlighted sentence in the passage? *Incorrect* choices change the meaning in important ways or leave out essential information.

    (A) Some predators have learned to distinguish between camouflaged moths and real leaves or twigs.

    (B) Moths' defenses have been so successful that other forest animals are evolving to adopt them.

    (C) Many moths camouflage themselves more realistically than they need to, given the poor eyesight of their predators.

    (D) Because moths are frequently viewed from close up by predators, their disguises must be very lifelike.

13. Directions: An introductory sentence for a brief summary of the passage is provided below. Complete the summary by selecting the THREE answer choices that express the most important ideas in the passage. Some sentences do not belong in the summary because they express ideas that are not presented in the passage or are minor details in the passage. This question is worth 2 points.

        Moths have several strategies that they use to survive, despite their inability to fight back well against predators.

        •

        •

        •

Answer Choices	
Adult moths can fly, so they can make themselves less identifiable through mimicry or surprise a predator with chemicals.	As long as caterpillars can distract predators temporarily, they usually have time to crawl to safety.
Moths perform useful functions, so it is worth it for humans to protect them from harm.	Markings that are frightening to predators are often beautiful to humans who study moths.
Pupae cannot move, so they remain out of sight or rely on caterpillars to ward off predators.	Predators avoid poisonous insects, so moths that are poisonous find it easier to survive.

Reading Drill #7

Julia Morgan's Architecture

Julia Morgan, a shy, soft-spoken woman, is regarded by some as the United States' most successful female architect. In 1894, she was the first woman to complete the University of California's Civil Engineering program. After she received her undergraduate degree, one of her professors recommended that she travel to the Ecole des Beaux-Arts in Paris to continue her education in architecture.

When she arrived in Paris, Morgan was initially refused entry to the school as no woman had been accepted there before. Undeterred, she entered and won several prestigious architectural competitions in Europe. Armed with newfound recognition and with letters of recommendation from several prominent figures in the field of architecture, Morgan applied again to the Ecole des Beaux Arts and was accepted in 1898. Four years later she completed her studies and returned to Oakland, California, to begin immediate work on several projects at Berkeley. The first woman to receive a state architect's license in California, she opened her own office in San Francisco just two years later, beginning an illustrious career that was to span almost fifty years, until the office's closing in 1950.

Few people outside architectural circles have heard of Julia Morgan because she loathed personal publicity and did everything in her power to avoid celebrity. She shunned the press and refused to allow her name to be posted at construction sites. Constant battles with ear infections affected her balance and made it difficult for her to walk evenly. Tragically, in the 1920s, complications resulting from surgery on her inner ear left her face asymmetrical. Her physical awkwardness only encouraged her innate reclusive tendencies and pushed her further from the public eye. When she retired, she ordered all of her papers burned, believing that an architect should be like the usually anonymous medieval master builders who created Europe's vast monasteries, cathedrals, and castles. In Morgan's view, a building should speak for itself. The structures she designed—notably Berkeley's Hearst Greek Theater, Baptist Divinity School and Hearst Memorial Mining Building, along with a number of other college facilities and residential houses—are elegant testimony to her brilliant architectural vision.

Known as a rare architect with little ego (she never rejected a project because it had a small budget), Morgan was interested neither in innovation for its own sake nor in developing a style readily identifiable as her own. Instead, she focused on the insides of her buildings, making interiors that were elegantly simple, while the exteriors were sober and carefully balanced. Keeping with the philosophy of the Beaux-Arts movement that architecture should focus on and cater to the individual, Morgan strove to build structures that were practical to live and work in. Accordingly, a large percentage of her work consisted of residential commissions. She frequently collaborated with the late Walter Steilberg, a respected architect himself who served as her structural engineer. Steilberg once commented that her "object was first of all to build a home." Her house designs demonstrated respect for the everyday needs of the residents.

An honorary Doctor of Laws degree awarded by the University of California at Berkeley in 1929 well summarizes her mark on the American cultural landscape: "Designer of simple dwellings and stately homes, of great buildings nobly planned to further the centralized activities of her fellow citizens; Architect in whose works harmony and admirable proportions bring pleasure to the eye and peace to the mind." **With its pleasing straightforwardness and lack of waste, Morgan's style warrants more attention than it sometimes receives in the world of contemporary architecture, which values extravagance.** And in a field still dominated by men over a hundred years after her birth, her lifetime of achievement—a record of over 700 completed projects spanning residences, institutions, churches, estates, and community buildings—stands as an inspiration to young women entering careers in architecture.

1. What does the passage mainly discuss?

    (A)   The professional work of Julia Morgan
    (B)   Julia Morgan's knowledge of architectural history
    (C)   The influence of structural engineering on Julia Morgan's career
    (D)   Julia Morgan's role in the women's movement

2. The word shunned in the passage is closest in meaning to

    (A)   avoided
    (B)   spoke to
    (C)   embraced
    (D)   misunderstood

3. What happened to Julia Morgan's papers?

    (A)   They were donated to a university.
    (B)   They were sold to an engineering firm.
    (C)   They were destroyed.
    (D)   They were stored in a vault.

4. The phrase speak for itself in the passage is closest in meaning to

    (A)   communicate verbally
    (B)   be designed to carry sound well
    (C)   demonstrate its own qualities
    (D)   be good publicity for its architect

5. It can be inferred from the passage that Julia Morgan paid little attention to which of the following?

    (A)   The wishes of her clients
    (B)   The quality of her buildings
    (C)   Her income
    (D)   Her privacy

6. Click on the sentence in paragraph 4 that refers to Julia Morgan's attitude toward the people for whom she built houses.

7. The word object in the passage is closest in meaning to

    (A) process
    (B) material
    (C) goal
    (D) sensitivity

8. It can be inferred from the passage that Julia Morgan

    (A) collaborated with many other architects
    (B) made a lot of money
    (C) had a distinctive personal style of design
    (D) wanted her buildings to be useful

9. The author quotes Walter Steilberg in order to

    (A) disprove a theory
    (B) describe his work
    (C) support a previous statement
    (D) give detail about one of Morgan's projects

10. What does the passage imply about other well-known architects besides Morgan?

    (A) Most were more innovative than Morgan.
    (B) Many have also emulated the medieval masters in their designs.
    (C) Some have also burned their personal papers upon retiring.
    (D) Many have large egos.

11. The passage describes Julia Morgan's buildings as

    (A) old-fashioned
    (B) large
    (C) simple
    (D) innovative

12. Which of the sentences below best expresses the essential information in the bolded sentence in the passage? *Incorrect* choices change the meaning in important ways or leave out essential information.

   (A)   Many of Morgan's buildings could not be built today because they would be too expensive.
   (B)   The simplicity of Morgan's buildings is currently undervalued, but she deserves a higher reputation.
   (C)   Contemporary architects are rediscovering Morgan's designs as an influence on their own buildings.
   (D)   Morgan was very honest about her dislike for most contemporary architecture.

13. According to the passage, which of the following contributed to Morgan's shyness?

   (A)   The many fans who followed her everywhere
   (B)   Her negative reputation with the press
   (C)   The results of a failed surgery
   (D)   The fire that destroyed her papers

Reading Drill #8

Colonial Glass

The first items manufactured in the North American colonies of England were glasswares; in fact the first colonial glass factory was established in 1607 in Virginia. However, it required nearly two centuries more for the industry to begin truly flourishing. Some of the problems were on the supply side: the government limited production of glass in the colonies. This policy was designed to ensure that the colonists would continue to buy glass made in England, with money and raw materials thus constantly flowing back toward the mother country.

There were problems on the demand side also. Because glassmaking was, for all intents and purposes, prohibited, techniques did not develop rapidly. Colonists who were affluent enough to afford expensive glass items associated English and European products with sophistication and luxury. American glass was thought to be practical but somewhat crude. That perception changed slowly, but it began to shift around the time of the American Revolution. Shortly before the war began in the 1770s, a German immigrant brought knowledge of lead crystal making to the colony of Pennsylvania. Lead crystal was not a mineral crystal but was made from melted and cooled sand, like other glass. Mixing in small amounts of lead made the glass clear and soft enough to be cut into patterns that reflected light attractively, a technique long associated with the skilled craftsmen of the European cities of Venice and Prague. The Pennsylvania immigrant established the idea that locally made glass could be beautiful as well as functional, thus beginning the process of winning over consumers with money to spend on expensive glassware.

Nevertheless, several subsequent developments were required to produce the flowering of glassmaking in America in the late nineteenth century. One was America's abundance of the fine-grade sand suitable to be used in glass, which drove its price down. Additionally, technology advanced in key ways. Traditional glassmaking had relied on furnaces powered with coal or wood; controlling the heat for the purposes of glassmaking was labor-intensive. As new furnaces powered by natural gas and electricity came into use, temperature control became much easier, allowing glassmakers unprecedented consistency of quality. New tools for cutting and processing glass after it left the furnace were also invented. These tools produced many of the effects of old hand-cutting, but they required less skill (and therefore less investment in time and money) to use. These improvements in materials and technology came about just as the number of consumers wealthy and discriminating enough to demand high-quality glass was increasing rapidly.

The leading and cutting of glass was not the only technique that flourished from the 1850s through the 1920s, and in fact, other types of glassware are considered even more traditionally American by many. Milk glass, so called because it is translucent white rather than clear and slightly blue like natural glass, was often pressed into patterns rather than cut. Milk glass had been devised centuries earlier in Europe as an inexpensive substitute for the porcelain imported from China. **The innovation of American manufacturers was to treat it as a material with pleasing properties of its own instead, freeing their imaginations to mold it into new shapes and designs.** Conversely, the controlled production of the clear, colorless glass familiar to us also became possible during this period. With new technology, the use of mineral additives to make clear glass with an intense green, blue, or yellow color became possible. Such glass became very popular among consumers. And these two

American specialties—milk glass and tinted clear glass—could be combined. The process used to make milk glass could, with different chemical additives, yield an almost black glass whose edges glowed purple in strong light. At its zenith, glassware from America was of the highest quality being produced at the time.

1. Which of the following subjects does the passage mainly discuss?

    (A) Popular patterns of American cut glass
    (B) How the glassmaking industry developed in America
    (C) Countries from which America received glassmaking technology
    (D) Methods for producing colored glass

2. Which of the following is an example of problems on the demand side?

    (A) The reputation of local glass among American colonists
    (B) The inability of local glassmakers to produce milk glass
    (C) Lack of sophistication among American consumers
    (D) British controls on glassmaking in the colonies

3. The word affluent in the passage is closest in meaning to

    (A) numerous
    (B) foreign
    (C) rich
    (D) artistic

4. The word perception in the passage is closest in meaning to

    (A) impression
    (B) discovery
    (C) movement
    (D) education

5. The word subsequent in the passage is closest in meaning to

    (A) traditional
    (B) necessary
    (C) following
    (D) exciting

6.   The word properties in the passage refers to

     (A)   the distances separating China from Europe and America
     (B)   the buildings required to manufacture glass
     (C)   the possessions of families that collected glass
     (D)   the characteristics of a kind of glass

7.   Paragraph 3 of the passage indicates that technological advancements made glassmaking require

     (A)   higher temperatures
     (B)   less skill
     (C)   smaller amounts of sand
     (D)   less cooling time

8.   Before colorless glass could be made, American natural glass was usually

     (A)   white
     (B)   yellow
     (C)   purple
     (D)   blue

9.   Paragraph 4 answers which of the following questions?

     (A)   What mineral is added to sand to make milk glass?
     (B)   How was European milk glass made to look like porcelain?
     (C)   How could patterns be added to glasswares without cutting?
     (D)   Which European countries produced the best glass after 1850?

10. Which of the following is NOT a development that increased the popularity of American-made glass?

     (A)   good-quality sand
     (B)   better cutting tools
     (C)   wealthier consumers
     (D)   less competition

11. Click on the paragraph in the passage that describes how glass cutting was first brought to the American colonies.

12. Which of the sentences below best expresses the essential information in the highlighted sentence in the passage? *Incorrect* choices change the meaning in important ways or leave out essential information.

(A) Some of the new designs glassmakers devised were more suited to Chinese porcelain than to milk glass.
(B) American glassmakers made milk glass that imitated Chinese porcelain even better than before.
(C) Glassmakers began using the distinctive beauty of milk glass to create new products rather than thinking of it as an imitation of something else.
(D) Because milk glass could be molded more easily than Chinese porcelain, it could be used in a greater variety of new designs.

13. Directions: An introductory sentence for a brief summary of the passage is provided below. Complete the summary by selecting the THREE answer choices that express the most important ideas in the passage. Some sentences do not belong in the summary because they express ideas that are not presented in the passage or are minor details in the passage. This question is worth 2 points.

American glassmaking developed slowly but eventually became the best in the world.

-
-
-

Answer Choices
America's high-quality sand and advances in technology allowed glassmaking to improve as demand increased.	Natural glass is not perfectly clear because of impurities in the sand from which it is made.
Some people prefer glass made with traditional furnaces and tools, despite difficulties of quality control.	A combination of British policy and prejudice among potential local buyers discouraged the development of glassmaking in the colonies.
Glassmakers developed types of products, ranging from milk glass to clear colored glass, that were the finest of their kind.	The most advanced centers of glass production at the time were Venice and Prague.

Reading Drill #9

Developments in Transportation

Transportation costs in the United States account for over 20 percent of the gross national product. It also accounts for almost 40 percent of the total amount of energy consumed. Most trains, airplanes, and automobiles use petroleum-based fuels. And even vehicles that run on electricity or alternative fuels are constructed using processes that consume fossil fuels. In fact, despite improvements in design, the amount of money and energy spent on transportation increases every year.

This should not be surprising, given the extent to which the contemporary economy depends on rapid distribution of goods and services. Until the middle of the twentieth century, mass production was accomplished through centralized, large-scale factories. Similarly, goods were distributed nationwide via a limited number of giant warehouses. This system minimized production costs but required large inventories.

Companies today prefer just-in-time delivery systems, meaning that items are delivered as needed to cut down the expense and effort of storing them for long periods. The smaller quantities of goods delivered in such a system require a greater number of smaller warehouses, and they also require transportation by truck. Since 1950, train transport of freight has fallen more than 60 percent. Truck transportation cuts down on the amount of time needed to plan a shipment, but it also consumes more energy than instead of cheaper and more efficient rail systems. Transporting a ton of goods by truck consumes four times as much energy as transporting the same ton by train over the same distance.

The increase in the use of trucks for delivery of goods has paralleled the increase in automobile use for personal transportation. Not only do more people own cars now than at any point in history, but they also live farther away from their place of work. This means that more nonrenewable resources are used every day. The average commute now takes more than forty-five minutes, more than it took a century ago when city-dwellers lived near the jobs they commuted to and could take public transportation such as trolley cars. This places a greater strain not only on the economy, but also on the environment. The emissions from millions of automobiles send a flood of pollutants into the air above major industrial areas and cause health problems. These emissions may also be contributing to global warming.

Because of these stresses caused by changes in the use of transportation, many cities are now considering more extensive public transportation projects. Recognizing that more than half of their downtown land area is devoted to the movement and storage of automobiles, cities are taking steps to improve public transportation in order to use valuable space more efficiently. The average American now spends more per year on an automobile than on food. Therefore, resolutions by city governments to make public transportation more accessible may benefit private as well as public life.

There is a problem, however. Just as businesses prefer to use flexible distribution systems with truck rather than train shipments, people in general have not shown a willingness to give up their automobiles, which allow for individual freedom of movement in ways trains cannot. Voters in the city of Portland, Oregon, approved the formation of a land-use and transportation board with the power to set policies that would decrease traffic congestion and make development less chaotic. (The population of metropolitan Portland is expanding rapidly.) However, even the most optimistic projections of its planners indicate that its light-rail train system and traffic measures are likely to decrease automobile use by only 5%. One problem is that strategies such as Portland's generally involve raising population densities, often through zoning policies that require multi-unit housing or commercial buildings. Putting people and their destinations closer together does decrease the distances they must travel by car, but it increases the number of people using the same roads. In other words, traffic congestion rises, and travel times may not decrease significantly.

1. The author of the passage is mainly arguing that

    (A) more people want access to public transportation
    (B) the number of transportation methods available has increased recently
    (C) transportation problems exist mostly in cities
    (D) changes in transportation patterns cause economic and other problems

2. Why does the author mention just-in-time delivery systems?

    (A) They have caused greater energy consumption.
    (B) Most people find them difficult to use.
    (C) They are commonly used only in cities.
    (D) People who drive automobiles don't understand them.

3. The word consumes is closest in meaning to which of the following?

    (A) Brings along
    (B) Represents
    (C) Uses up
    (D) Contains

4. Paragraph 4 suggests that the increased length of commutes to work

    (A) has increased the speed at which goods are delivered
    (B) was caused by an increase in the use of public transportation
    (C) is more noticeable outside large cities
    (D) has possible environmental consequences

5. The author argues that commuters use more nonrenewable resources today because

    (A) there are more inefficient automobiles on the road
    (B) more people must drive farther to work than before
    (C) many drivers are less considerate of energy resources
    (D) automotive technology has not advanced quickly enough

6. The highlighted word they refers to

   (A) truck drivers
   (B) economists
   (C) jobs
   (D) city-dwellers

7. According to the passage, a problem caused by increased automobile emissions is

   (A) coastal flooding
   (B) slowed transportation
   (C) poor air quality
   (D) urban fires

8. Which of the following conclusions is best supported by the passage?

   (A) Americans spend a considerable amount on transportation.
   (B) Many transportation costs can be eliminated through improved roads.
   (C) City planning will not decrease automobile cost.
   (D) Modern cars are less efficient than automobiles manufactured 40 years ago.

9. The phrase devoted to in the passage is closest in meaning to

   (A) used for
   (B) famous for
   (C) unavailable for
   (D) understood as

10. The word resolutions in the passage is closest in meaning to

    (A) increases
    (B) decisions
    (C) statistics
    (D) buildings

11. Why are cities increasing efforts to provide public transportation?

    (A) Commuting times are very long.
    (B) Using cars requires a lot of land.
    (C) People have complained about air pollution from cars.
    (D) Cars are expensive to maintain.

12. According to the passage, a problem with the city of Portland's planning is that it

    (A) does not provide enough rail lines
    (B) lowers population density
    (C) makes traffic worse
    (D) goes against the wishes of voters

13. Directions: An introductory sentence for a brief summary of the passage is provided below. Complete the summary by selecting the THREE answer choices that express the most important ideas in the passage. Some sentences do not belong in the summary because they express ideas that are not presented in the passage or are minor details in the passage. This question is worth 2 points.

Increased use of the automobile for transportation has produced both advantages and disadvantages.

-
-
-

Answer Choices	
Public transportation options include not only light rail trains but also electric trolley cars.	Delivering goods by truck requires more energy while making scheduling more flexible.
People prefer the freedom of traveling by car despite traffic congestion and high energy consumption.	Most freight used to be transported by train to large warehouses in a few key locations.
Research indicates that development planning can increase population densities while decreasing traffic congestion.	Cities such as Portland have not created policies that strike a balance between saving resources and pleasing consumers.

Reading Drill #10

Cowboys

The cowhand or cowboy, a famed and colorful figure, was the master of the long drive and the roundup. The first cowhands originally hailed from Mexico. These *vaqueros*, the Spanish term for cowboy, invented almost all the tools of the cowhand's trade, from the distinctive hat and rope lariat to the special saddle. The debt owed by American cowboys to the early Mexican innovators is apparent in such Spanish-derived terms as lasso, corral, and ranch. Even the famed rodeo is derived from the Spanish *charreada*.

The cowhand's life was an arduous one. Cowhands worked sunup to sundown and received lower wages than most factory workers. Their legs became bowed from long days in the saddle, and many developed permanent squints from looking into the glaring sunlight of the treeless plains. Wind, rain, sand, and strong sunlight toughened the skin over time but also caused injury. Because the job took such a physical toll on the body, most cowboys were young men in their teens and 20's, and it was unusual for a cowboy to last more than ten years in the job.

Given the rapid travel and physical exertion required of cowhands in these conditions, every item worn or carried served a necessary function. The wide brim of the "ten-gallon hat" could be turned down to shade the eyes or drain off rain that collected during rides over open terrain. Cowboys also could use their hats to carry water from a stream or to fan a slow-starting fire. The bandanna, a large handkerchief, could be tied over the nose and mouth to keep out all the dust raised by the running of countless cattle or it could used to protect the neck from sunburn. It also served as a towel, a napkin, and a bandage. Cowhands sometimes wore leather trousers called chaps over regular overalls. They protected the legs from injury if a rider fell from a horse or had to ride through cactus, sagebrush, or other thorny plants.

On a long drive, the central figure who planned the route and led the cowboys was the trail boss. The trail boss also selected his team of riders, so he had to be both a good judge of character and a good handler of various personalities. The figure with the second highest pay after the trail boss, and above the average cowboy, was the cook. The cook was sometimes a veteran cowboy who had been injured and who could no longer ride, or who had simply gotten old and grown weary of the long days in the saddle. **A good cook was essential to a successful drive, as the morale of the men often depended on him, and he was called upon to play doctor, nurse, and even barber.**

The cook rode in a wagon called the "chuckwagon," an innovation attributed to Charles Goodnight. In 1866, Goodnight rebuilt an army wagon and placed a cupboard in its rear. It was usually stocked with non-perishable food items, such as cornmeal, smoked bacon, pinto beans, molasses, and coffee. In addition to transporting food supplies, the chuckwagon also carried a large water barrel, firewood for cooking, and much of the cowboys' gear.

Today, much cowhanding is done from the safety and comfort of a pickup truck, rather than from horseback, so the danger of injury is low and supplies are accessible. But although the life of a cowhand is less picturesque and less romantic than it once was, it still involves the solitude that is so much a part of its traditional image.

1. The word colorful in paragraph 1 is used to indicate that cowboys

   (A) are no longer famous
   (B) wore bright clothes
   (C) were interesting
   (D) liked their work

2. The author mentions factory workers in paragraph 2 to indicate that

   (A) the work of a cowhand was not the most difficult
   (B) cowhands made little money
   (C) some cowhands changed to better jobs
   (D) equipment for cowhands was machine-made

3. The passage states that cowhands injured their eyes by

   (A) falling into thorny plants
   (B) looking toward the sun
   (C) keeping them open during sand storms
   (D) wiping them with dirty bandannas

4. It can be inferred that the cowhands mentioned in the passage worked primarily

   (A) in the mountains
   (B) in the forests
   (C) on the beaches
   (D) on the plains

5. The author uses the term countless in the passage to illustrate that the cattle

   (A) were numerous
   (B) were few
   (C) were unrestrained
   (D) were difficult to control

6. According to the passage, bandannas were used as all of the following EXCEPT

   (A) towels
   (B) napkins
   (C) bandages
   (D) trousers

7. The word They in paragraph 3 refers to

    (A)   overalls
    (B)   cowhands
    (C)   chaps
    (D)   horses

8. According to the passage, what was an important quality for a trail boss to have?

    (A)   Good endurance of the sun and wind
    (B)   The ability to cook well
    (C)   The ability to work with people
    (D)   Medical training to help injured cowboys

9. It can be inferred from the passage that cowhands did all of the following as part of their jobs EXCEPT

    (A)   make their own equipment
    (B)   round up cattle
    (C)   ride horses
    (D)   work through long drives

10. Which of the following can be inferred from the passage?

    (A)   Cattle came to the United States from Mexico.
    (B)   Some cowboy equipment originated outside the United States.
    (C)   Many cowhands had previously worked in factories.
    (D)   Women have always worked as cowhands.

11. The passage mentions the safety and comfort of a pickup truck in order to demonstrate

    (A)   that cowhands have been slow to accept modern equipment
    (B)   why some cowboys still prefer to work on horseback
    (C)   that the chuckwagon is no longer necessary
    (D)   that cowboys' work has become easier

12. Which of the sentences below best expresses the essential information in the bolded sentence in the passage? *Incorrect* choices change the meaning in important ways or leave out essential information.

   (A) The job of the cook could be filled by people who had been trained in other areas.
   (B) The role of the cook involved taking care of the cowboys in ways that went beyond making their meals.
   (C) The cook was often so busy attending to cowboys' personal needs that he had little time to prepare food.
   (D) The cook supervised a staff of several people who oversaw the health and welfare of the cowboys.

13. Directions: An introductory sentence for a brief summary of the passage is provided below. Complete the summary by selecting the THREE answer choices that express the most important ideas in the passage. Some sentences do not belong in the summary because they express ideas that are not presented in the passage or are minor details in the passage. This question is worth 2 points.

   The cowboy deserves his reputation for doing difficult work under harsh conditions.

   -
   -
   -

Answer Choices	
Some words for cowboy equipment were adopted from the Spanish used by Mexican cowboys.	The trail boss was in charge of choosing both the route and the employees for a long drive.
Cowboys required items of protective clothing to avoid the damaging effects of weather and desert plants.	Long drives were conducted with a minimum of equipment and few workers to take care of the cowboys.
Cowboys' work was so physically demanding that it damaged their legs and skin.	More people are interested in becoming cowhands now that modern equipment can be used.

Reading Drill #11

The Ruins of Angkor

The ruins of the temples of Angkor Wat are among the most impressive in the world. Located in modern day Cambodia near Tonlé Sap, the largest freshwater lake in Southeast Asia, the city of Angkor was the seat of power for the Khmer Empire from the ninth to fifteenth centuries. In their imposing scale, the ruins rival the pyramids of Giza in Egypt. The main complex consists of five giant towers, thought to symbolize sacred mountains. The tallest tower is 215 meters. It also contains the longest continuous bas-relief (a kind of carving) in the world. But even in its details—its galleries, pillars, and moats—Angkor Wat indicates that the empire that created it was highly advanced and powerful. It remains one of the most popular tourist destinations in all of Southeast Asia today.

Why this thriving civilization died out is a question that archaeologists are only beginning to ponder. There appear to be four main reasons. The first has to do with its irrigation system. The temples and palaces of Angkor were constructed around a series of artificial reservoirs and canals, which were annually flooded to capacity by the Mekong River. Once filled, they were used to irrigate the surrounding rice paddies and farmland over the course of the year. Farmers depended completely on this water for their rice crop. Large-scale farming around Tonlé Sap was impossible without irrigation.

Scientists speculate that an increasing population may have demanded greater food production from farmers just as the irrigation system they used was weakening with age. The construction of hundreds of sandstone temples and palaces required an enormous amount of physical labor. This meant that there were workers from the countryside pouring into Angkor, while the city's native population was also growing. The result was that the demand for food skyrocketed so quickly it outstripped the ability of the irrigation system to satisfy it. Efforts by farmers to increase productivity of rice also overworked the soil, leading to erosion and nutrient depletion.

Other factors relate to society and politics rather than physical infrastructure. The building of the massive irrigation system, temples, and other monuments required that the common people be practically enslaved to the ruling family, other aristocrats, and high-ranking priests. The religion they followed was a blend of Hinduism and Mahayana Buddhism that, not surprisingly, emphasized submission to authority. However, another branch of Buddhism (called Theravada) began spreading through Southeast Asia, and it preached the individual pursuit of enlightenment. The popularity of this doctrine decreased the incentive to obey the higher classes without questioning. The labor to support massive public works projects became difficult to obtain.

This was true not only within the city of Angkor but in the outlying provinces as well. Fueled partially by the spread of Theravada Buddhism, these provinces began to assert their independence, and some refused to pay their traditional tribute to the king. With less wealth coming into the city, there was lower funding for the maintenance and building of infrastructure just as the existing irrigation systems were showing strain.

But it was external pressure that may have been the death blow for the city of Angkor. The Khmer Empire had the misfortune to lie between the rising Thai and Vietnamese empires. Their power grew as the line of Khmer kings became less dynamic and powerful and its grip on its far-flung provinces slackened. In fact, the city was attacked and looted by the Thai in 1431, but it is known to have returned to use thereafter. In succeeding centuries, however, the city suffered alternating invasions by the Thai and Vietnamese armies, and Angkor's role as a center of civilization was lost.

1. The word seat in the passage is closest in meaning to

   (A) center
   (B) expansion
   (C) division
   (D) image

2. The author mentions the pyramids of Giza in order to

   (A) compare the Khmer Empire to another agricultural civilization
   (B) show that large structures were not only built near lakes
   (C) demonstrate the power of the Khmer Empire
   (D) indicate the size of Angkor Wat

3. Which of the following best describes the author's attitude toward Angkor Wat?

   (A) respect
   (B) indifference
   (C) pity
   (D) fear

4. The author suggests that archaeologists

   (A) are not impressed by the size of ruins of Angkor Wat
   (B) are only beginning to study Asia
   (C) leave studies of ancient agriculture to scholars in other fields
   (D) did not previously study the end of the Khmer Empire

5. The word thriving in the passage is closest in meaning to

   (A) prosperous
   (B) advanced
   (C) widespread
   (D) famous

6. According to the passage, which of the following is true of the land around Tonlé Sap?

   (A) It contains too much salt for large-scale farming.
   (B) It has not been farmed since the end of the Khmer Empire.
   (C) It is not naturally suited to the agriculture that Angkor required.
   (D) There are no rivers or streams flowing through it.

7. To which of the following does the word they in the passage refer?

   (A) Temples and palaces
   (B) Reservoirs and canals
   (C) Rice paddies
   (D) Farmers

8. Which of the following does the passage mention as a reason for rapid population growth in Angkor?

   (A) Workers moved into the city for building projects.
   (B) Farmers had more children as they became more prosperous.
   (C) People moved in to escape the yearly flooding of the Mekong River.
   (D) Farmers needed more laborers to increase soil productivity.

9. Which of the following is NOT discussed as a result of farmers' attempts to farm more productively?

   (A) Soil erosion
   (B) Population increases
   (C) Nutrient depletion
   (D) Excess demand for water

10. Which of the following can be inferred about the downfall of the Khmer Empire?

    (A) It was the only cause of population loss in Angkor.
    (B) Repair of the irrigation system would have prevented it.
    (C) It occurred before that of ancient Egypt.
    (D) Scientists are not yet certain what caused it.

11. The word outstripped in the passage is closest in meaning to

    (A) demonstrated
    (B) eliminated
    (C) exceeded
    (D) renewed

12. Paragraph 4 of the passage implies that the spread of Theravada Buddhism

    (A) caused the high-ranking priests to rebel
    (B) made the ruling family less interested in building large monuments
    (C) made the common people less willing to do hard labor
    (D) required the building of different kinds of temples

13. Directions: An introductory sentence for a brief summary of the passage is provided below. Complete the summary by selecting the THREE answer choices that express the most important ideas in the passage. Some sentences do not belong in the summary because they express ideas that are not presented in the passage or are minor details in the passage. This question is worth 2 points.

There are several factors that could explain the decline of the city of Angkor.

-
-
-

Answer Choices	
The city was not deserted suddenly but rather over a period of centuries.	The invading Thai Empire destroyed everything in the city besides the Angkor Wat complex.
The people of the countryside stopped giving labor and tribute to the Khmer rulers.	Invasions by neighboring societies weakened the political power of the Khmer Empire.
Excessive farming caused the soil and the irrigation system to deteriorate.	Researchers are still not sure how Khmer laborers could have produced the larger structures of the Angkor Wat complex.

Reading Drill #12

Paracelsus's Contribution to Medicine

The sixteenth-century physician Paracelsus not only made key scientific discoveries, but also changed medicine philosophically. Thanks to Paracelsus, the field became more accepting of new truths.

Early studies of human anatomy were seriously hampered by factors not directly related to the difficulty of understanding the structures of the body. The government disapproved of **dissections**. Additionally, the lack of refrigeration prevented dead bodies from being preserved for long periods before study. It was possible to use **chemical embalming** of bodies to preserve them, but the process altered their physical characteristics in ways that decreased their usefulness for study.

However, physicians did the best they could with available tools, and by the 1500s in Europe, the collected knowledge about the human body had been organized into a set of texts. This set was the exclusive property of the Doctors of Physick, a group of scholars who had a vested interest in keeping their knowledge rare and expensive. By maintaining reference works in ancient Latin (or sometimes ancient Greek and Arabic), which most outsiders could not read, the Doctors of Physick prevented others from questioning their beliefs and treatments. So conservative were the Doctors of Physick that they refused to use their day-to-day observations to supplement or revise existing texts. They also charged extravagant amounts to administer treatments to patients.

These treatments were of two main types: **blood lettings** for those with physiological disorders, and **point-branding** for those in need of psychiatric care. Blood lettings were frequently performed by attaching leeches to patients with physical complaints; the parasitic creatures would suck blood through the skin until they swelled and detached themselves. For patients with complaints about the mind rather than the body, point-brandings were performed with heated needles. Both treatments were said to draw out various poisons. In reality, these treatments were effective only for limited types of ailments. When applied inappropriately, these treatments had no effect or actually worsened the condition of a patient. Understandably, many common people opted to get medicines from village apothecaries. The herbal remedies provided by apothecaries were also often ineffective, but at least they didn't make the sick feel worse.

It was in these circumstances that Paracelsus began practicing medicine. Paracelsus was a self-taught medicine man who took a practical approach to medicine, rather than following the traditions that had grown up around it. He instructed his own students at the University of Basel in a local dialect instead of Latin, for example. He taught based on his own experience as a doctor who had treated hundreds of patients rather than using inaccurate but time-honored models. **He went so far as to burn books of medical principles valued by the Doctors of Physick because he found them meaningless when applied to patients.**

Other professors were angered at his way of making medical knowledge practical and accessible to outsiders. This violated the Hippocratic oath, in which the Doctor of Physick swore to guard his professional knowledge. Given his record of, time after time, putting a higher priority on a straightforward understanding of medicine than on respect for tradition, it was no surprise when Paracelsus was ejected from the university in 1528. His philosophy, however, had begun to have its effect and could not be stopped. The effect was strengthened after his death, when his works were published. Paracelsus's careful observation of his many patients compensated for the inability to study preserved bodies. One of his key contributions to medical knowledge was rejecting the belief that disease was caused by a lack of balance among fluids, called "humors," within a patient's body. But this was just the beginning of the far-reaching impact Paracelsus had on Western medicine.

1. What is the passage mainly about?

    (A) A scientist's contribution to the field of medicine
    (B) The causes of disease in the body
    (C) How doctors learn anatomy by treating patients
    (D) The European university system in the sixteenth century

2. The word key in the passage is closest in meaning to

    (A) interesting
    (B) unknown
    (C) complicated
    (D) important

3. Why did the Doctors of Physick not allow writings in contemporary languages?

    (A) Contemporary languages lacked words to describe certain parts of the body.
    (B) They had spent time and money learning Latin.
    (C) Books in contemporary languages were expensive to produce.
    (D) Common people could not read medical writings in Latin.

4. The author mentions that the government disapproved of dissections as an example of

    (A) a reason it was difficult to study anatomy
    (B) an organization that cooperated with the Doctors of Physick
    (C) an organization that supported Paracelsus's new discoveries
    (D) the difficulties of finding money to pay for new research

5. Which **phrase in bold text** in the passage identifies a treatment that was used for mental problems? (Scroll the passage to see all of the answer choices.)

6. It can be inferred from the passage that the Doctors of Physick

    (A) only treated the richest patients
    (B) were looking for ways to preserve bodies for study
    (C) had little experience treating patients
    (D) did not always help their patients feel better

7.   The word opted in the passage is closest in meaning to

     (A)   avoided
     (B)   refused
     (C)   chose
     (D)   recommended

8.   According to the passage, what can be concluded about Paracelsus's medical education?

     (A)   His patients were rarely satisfied with his care.
     (B)   He educated himself about medicine.
     (C)   He was disliked by apothecaries.
     (D)   He guarded his medical knowledge closely.

9.   The passage implies that the Hippocratic oath included a promise to

     (A)   question traditional medical knowledge
     (B)   cooperate with village apothecaries
     (C)   prevent outsiders from learning about medicine
     (D)   consult frequently with other medical professors

10. The word ejected in the passage is closest in meaning to

     (A)   honored
     (B)   removed
     (C)   questioned
     (D)   studied

11. The paragraph following the passage most probably discusses

     (A)   the humors found in the human body
     (B)   how different cultures view disease
     (C)   additional ways Paracelsus influenced medicine
     (D)   typical conditions in sixteenth century hospitals

12. Which of the sentences below best expresses the essential information in the bolded sentence in the passage? *Incorrect* choices change the meaning in important ways or leave out essential information.

   (A) The Doctors of Physick were pleased when the notes Paracelsus had made about his patients were burned.
   (B) The Doctors of Physick asked Paracelsus to destroy books that they no longer felt were valuable.
   (C) Paracelsus burned the medical books he had written to prevent the Doctors of Physick from taking credit for them.
   (D) Paracelsus felt that the principles in existing medical books were so ineffective they should be destroyed.

13. Directions: An introductory sentence for a brief summary of the passage is provided below. Complete the summary by selecting the THREE answer choices that express the most important ideas in the passage. Some sentences do not belong in the summary because they express ideas that are not presented in the passage or are minor details in the passage. This question is worth 2 points.

   Paracelsus overcame obstacles to change both medical knowledge and the way medical knowledge was obtained.

   -
   -
   -

Answer Choices	
He made his medical theories accessible by teaching them to outsiders in contemporary languages.	He perfected a method of using leeches to draw out blood from wounds.
He based his treatments on actual experience with patients rather than tradition or the dissection of dead bodies.	He lost his position as a university professor, but his theories gained acceptance after his death.
He worked with village apothecaries to make reliable treatments affordable to the common people.	He revised the Hippocratic oath to include a promise not to harm patients.

Reading Drill #13

The Expansion of the Steel Industry

The railroad industry could not have grown as large as it did without the development of the steel industry. The first rails were made of iron, but iron rails were not strong enough to support heavy trains running at high speeds. Railroad executives wanted to replace them with steel rails because steel was ten to fifteen times as strong and lasted twenty times longer. Before the 1870s, however, steel was made using a slow and arduous process. Bars of Swedish wrought iron were typically heated together with charcoal over a period of six weeks, during which time the iron absorbed carbon from the charcoal. The bars were then broken into smaller pieces and melted down in relatively small-sized crucibles. Because of the costs and difficulties inherent in this drawn-out method of production, steel found only limited application. Ships, bridges, railroad rails, and axles were still constructed with wrought iron, while steel was only used for smaller items, such as cutlery, tools, and springs.

Given the superior performance of steel, it is not surprising that a number of inventors in Great Britain, the United States, and Germany were working to find a less expensive method of making it. Although several of them arrived independently at the same solution, it was Henry Bessemer who took credit in 1856 for discovering that directing a blast of heated air at melted iron in a furnace burned out the impurities that made the iron brittle, a process he named the Acid Bessemer process. When the fire cooled, the metal had been converted to steel. His machine, called the Bessemer converter, made possible the mass production of steel. The differences between the new and old processes were enormous. The cost of producing steel fell ten-fold, and whereas it had been made previously in blocks of 40 or 50 pounds each, three to five tons of iron could now be changed into steel in a matter of minutes. The effect on the railroads was immediate and enormous: all-steel rails, called Bessemer rails, quickly replaced those of hardened-head iron as the industry standard.

Just when the demand for more steel developed among manufacturers and transportation companies, its costs was driven down still further when prospectors discovered huge new deposits of iron ore in the mountains of the Mesabi Range in Minnesota near Lake Superior. ■ The Mesabi deposits were so near the surface that they could be mined with steam shovels. Barges and steamers carried the iron ore across Lake Superior to depots on the southern shores of Lake Michigan and Lake Erie. ■ With dizzying speed, disparate spots such as Gary, Indiana, and Toledo, Youngstown, and Cleveland, Ohio, became major steel-manufacturing centers. Pittsburgh, at the confluence of the Allegheny and Monongahela rivers in Western Pennsylvania, became the greatest steel city of all.

■ Steel rapidly became the basic building material of the industrial age, and railroads laid down with Bessemer rails helped shape the industrial development of the nation, as manufacturers east of the Mississippi River became connected at all times to the growing markets in the West. Before the nation became connected via railroad, transportation routes had depended heavily upon weather and season. In this regard, steel helped eliminate natural barriers to the progress of economic growth, and the economies of cities like Chicago grew prodigiously. Not only was steel used in crisscrossing the territory with railways, but also in punctuating the urban landscape with structures taller than what was previously thought possible. ■

Total production figures graphically illustrate the rapid proliferation of steel in the last three decades of the nineteenth century. In 1870 only 77,000 tons of steel were produced in America, but by the turn of the century thirty years later, annual production had mushroomed to over eleven million tons.

1. Which of the following is NOT mentioned in the passage as a reason that steel used to be expensive?

    (A) The process of making it was slow.
    (B) It had to be made in small quantities.
    (C) Some readily accessible supplies of iron had not been discovered.
    (D) Bessemer's machine was costly to operate.

2. The author mentions ships, bridges, railroad rails, and axles to indicate that steel

    (A) was superior to wrought iron in versatility
    (B) could be shipped efficiently to buyers
    (C) made mass transportation possible
    (D) was too expensive to use in large items

3. The phrase a matter of minutes in the passage indicates that steel

    (A) was converted in small amounts
    (B) was difficult to make
    (C) was manufactured for the first time
    (D) could be produced quickly

4. According to the passage, the railroad industry preferred steel to iron because steel was

    (A) cheaper
    (B) lighter
    (C) cleaner
    (D) sturdier

5. Which of the following is a reason given for the invention of the Bessemer furnace?

    (A) The expense of mining iron ore
    (B) The risks involved in producing steel
    (C) Bessemer's desire for fame
    (D) The high cost of steel

6. According to the passage, how did the Bessemer method make the mass production of steel possible?

   (A) It removed impurities efficiently.
   (B) It slowly heated large quantities of iron.
   (C) It made iron into a substitute for steel.
   (D) It located deposits of iron ore.

7. The word independently in the passage is closest in meaning to

   (A) cleverly
   (B) separately
   (C) quickly
   (D) officially

8. The Bessemer process of making steel from iron involved

   (A) steam shovels
   (B) repeated stirring
   (C) hot air
   (D) a chemical solution

9. The prospectors referred to in the passage were

   (A) owners of businesses that used steel
   (B) people who searched for sources of ore
   (C) inventors who wanted to make the manufacture of steel easier
   (D) owners of shipping companies

10. It can be inferred from the passage that the mass production of steel caused

   (A) a decline in the auto industry
   (B) a revolution in the industrial world
   (C) an increase in the price of steel
   (D) a feeling of discontent among steel workers

11. The word mushroomed in the passage is closest in meaning to which of the following?

   (A) became efficient
   (B) increased greatly
   (C) was calculated
   (D) was planned

12. Look at the four squares [■] that indicate where the following sentence could be added to the passage.

Later, it was also used in producing automobiles, which would decrease demand for rail transport.

Reading Drill #14

Locust Invasions

In the United States, before the agricultural development of the Midwest and West altered the natural balance of wildlife, there were frequent migrations of Rocky Mountain locusts (*Melanoplus spretus*) that caused terrible damage to local agricultural economies. Great hordes of these insects used to darken the skies on the plains east of the Rocky Mountains, often destroying crops. The following letter written by a Missouri farmer in 1875 graphically demonstrates the severity of the problem: "The locusts are taking every green thing as fast as it appears above the ground in this part of the county, say ten or twelve miles from the river. Beyond that I am told there is little small grain, vegetables and corn. Most of the county shows as little sign of vegetation as it did in March, except the trees. All the small fruit is gone, they have even eaten the weeds."

The worst period of locust migrations was from 1874 to 1877, and 1875 was the peak of the disaster. The seriousness of damage from the locusts in Nebraska is indicated by The Grasshopper Constitution, a revision of the original state constitution to include policies to reckon with the economic problems. **Similarly, the state of Missouri passed legislation in 1877 to stop the grasshopper crisis by authorizing a bounty on locusts and grasshoppers: anyone collecting a bushel of eggs was to be paid five dollars, while a bushel of young grasshoppers was worth one dollar.** Such measures, as could easily be predicted, were in vain, for at that time some swarms consisted of over 100 billion individual insects. **In Missouri alone, the estimate of the amount of damage to crops and land exceeded 15 million dollars.** In addition to grain, fruit, and vegetables, farmers were also losing livestock every day because of the lack of feed. This led to problems for the settlers themselves, who were starving and trying to survive merely with bread and water. Whole families of settlers were often discovered starved to death in their farmhouses.

The migratory locust swarms that cause that sort of devastation arise under extreme environmental pressures, such as overcrowding and climate changes. **These forms of locusts are apparently natural adaptations, designed to spread locust populations out when they become too crowded.** Fortunately for farmers today, the migratory locust, the so-called "spretus" species, no longer seems to occur regularly. Even so, there was a serious outbreak as late as 1938 in the Midwest of the United States and Canada. In fact, there is no reason to assume that the destructive migratory form would not appear again if circumstances became favorable.

Locust swarms are large and can lay waste to everything in their path, but despite the difficulties humans have in combating them, they are not unstoppable. Nature usually has ways of controlling the population of any given species, and locusts are no exception. For locusts, the primary control mechanisms are weather and natural predators. For example, the Rocky Mountain locust is native to regions of high altitude and low rainfall. When a swarm of Rocky Mountain locusts migrates into a different climate in search of food, it can be wiped out with astonishing speed by a few weeks of extreme temperatures and rain.

Locusts also have many natural predators. A special type of mite that likes to feed off young locusts by lodging under their wings is among the most significant. Spiders, dragonflies, and hair worms are other invertebrates that prey on locusts, and the chief vertebrate enemies of the Rocky Mountain locust are birds. Some researchers have found that there are birds in moist lowlands that live almost entirely on locusts during seasons of invasion.

1. The author quotes the farmer's letter in paragraph 1 of the passage to indicate

   (A) how frequently hordes of locusts caused damage in the Midwest and West
   (B) how far away from their place of origin the locusts traveled
   (C) the amount of plant life destroyed by the locusts
   (D) the season in which locust swarms were most frequent

2. The word altered in the passage is closest in meaning to

   (A) created
   (B) recognized
   (C) studied
   (D) changed

3. The author uses the phrase darken the skies in the passage to indicate that

   (A) locusts tended to migrate in rainy weather
   (B) migrations of locusts moved quickly
   (C) there were many locusts in a swarm
   (D) locust swarms moved up the mountains

4. Which of the sentences below best expresses the essential information in the highlighted sentence in the passage? *Incorrect* choices change the meaning in important ways or leave out essential information.

   (A) The revisions to the Nebraska constitution were insufficient to deal with the economic problems caused by locust plagues.
   (B) Nebraska was the only state to suffer significantly from locust plagues, as is recorded in its revised constitution.
   (C) The Nebraska constitution was rewritten to provide ways to deal with future locust plagues.
   (D) Nebraska suffered so much damage from locusts that its constitution had to be rewritten to deal with it.

5. The phrase reckon with in the passage is closest in meaning to

   (A) publicize
   (B) find the total
   (C) take money from
   (D) solve

6. Click on the sentence in paragraph 3 that states when the last outbreak of migratory locusts occurred.

7. The phrase lay waste in the passage is closest in meaning to

   (A) destroy
   (B) control
   (C) fly over
   (D) view

8. The word astonishing in the passage is closest in meaning to

   (A) wasteful
   (B) unexpected
   (C) theoretical
   (D) recorded

9. The passage implies that Rocky Mountain locusts cannot easily survive

   (A) high altitude
   (B) extreme temperatures
   (C) seasons of invasion
   (D) crowding

10. The author mentions spiders, dragonflies, and hair worms in the passage as invertebrates that

    (A) compete with locusts for food
    (B) are eaten by birds that eat locusts
    (C) help to control locust populations
    (D) are preyed on by locusts

11. The passage supports which of the following conclusions?

    (A) Nebraska has never recovered from the economic problems caused by locusts.
    (B) Migratory locusts have no vertebrate enemies.
    (C) Climate is a factor that influences locust migrations.
    (D) There is no artificial way to control damage from locust migrations.

12. Click on the sentence in **bold text** in the passage where the author explains the main purpose of locust migrations.

Reading Drill #15

The Kachina of the Native Americans

According to traditional beliefs of the Hopi and Pueblo tribes of the American Southwest, their villages are visited by kachina every year on the winter solstice. These kachina are thought to be the spirits of dead ancestors who have come down from their residences on the peaks of the San Francisco mountain range to spend half the year watching over the living.

Each kachina is said to possess not only a specific personality but also a lesson to **impart to** the members of the village. These personalities include chiefs who bring lessons of wisdom, women who teach motherly values, and demons or ogres who **attend to** serious issues of discipline and behavior. There are, however, also clown-like characters who bring **comic relief** to ceremonies that would otherwise be entirely solemn. Named the Koshari Kachina, or sometimes just clown or glutton, these figures act in outrageous ways that are meant to amuse the crowds. However, their presence also serves another more serious function. **By breaking various taboos and transgressing boundaries set up by society, the Koshari Kachina provide examples to the younger members of the tribe of unacceptable conduct.**

The Hopi and Pueblo incorporate representations of the kachina into both ceremonial and daily life for the duration of these visits. Ceremonial dance is a major display of their role. On the night of the winter solstice, dancers welcome the kachina back to human settlements by donning masks, each of which represents a particular spirit. This spirit possesses power, which it grants to the wearer of the mask. After their welcome by the tribespeople, the kachina are thought to stay with the village through the winter and spring months. Over this half-year period, many ceremonies are held in which the masked dancers assume the powers of the kachina and instruct the members of the village.

The kachina are also represented among the the Southwestern tribes through the use of dolls. Each doll, traditionally made from the root of the cottonwood tree, is carved in the image of a particular kachina and is believed to have a small bit of the kachina residing within it. The dolls represent stock characters in the kachina tradition and are easily identifiable by typical **motifs**. The Koshari Kachina, for example, is usually portrayed holding a slice of watermelon, a symbol of the clown's gluttonous nature. The Angak'China, or Long-Haired Kachina, is a common figure among almost all the Hopi and Pueblo tribes. He is considered a bringer of gentle rains, and the long hair running down his back is supposed to resemble falling rain. Other kachinas actually take the shape of plants or animals. The Patung Kachina, or Squash Kachina, is a humanoid form in the shape of a squash plant, a symbol of food. Mongwu, the Great Horned Owl Kochina, is an owl with an elaborately carved headdress of feathers. This kachina plays an important role in the dance ceremonies. His duty is to punish the clowns when their behavior becomes too outrageous and to bring order back from the chaos.

Nowadays, the most common practice for many doll-makers is to use long-lasting acrylic paints, but some have begun to return to traditional mineral and plant pigments. The dolls are made with great care. They are incised with intricate symbols and often carry accessories, such as arrows or baskets, and are highly valued by collectors. They have a special place of honor in Hopi and Pueblo homes, but the original role of the dolls is not precisely known. Some historians say that the first dolls were given to women and children merely as representatives of the spirits, while others believe that they were aids in teaching children about the kachina.

1. The phrase **impart to** in the passage is closest in meaning to which of the following?

    (A) enjoy with
    (B) fulfill
    (C) distinguish from
    (D) deliver to

2. The phrase **attend to** in the passage could best be replaced by

    (A) are unrelated with
    (B) warn about
    (C) are responsible for
    (D) add humor to

3. The purpose of paragraph 2 is to list

    (A) the kinds of kachina dolls that are commonly made
    (B) the tribe members who participate in kachina ceremonies
    (C) the roles of kachina characters
    (D) the lessons tribal chiefs learn from the kachina

4. The author uses the phrase comic relief in the passage to refer to

    (A) a lesson not normally attended to by the kachina
    (B) issues of discipline and behavior
    (C) a short break from the seriousness of the rest of the ceremonies
    (D) the way modern tribespeople view the tradition of the kachina

5. Which of the sentences below best expresses the essential information in the bolded sentence in the passage? *Incorrect* choices change the meaning in important ways or leave out essential information.

    (A) Because Koshari Kachina act out unacceptable conduct, children are not permitted to watch them perform.
    (B) The Koshari Kachina are used to teach children which behavior is considered bad by the community.
    (C) The Koshari Kachina are clown-like figures who comically imitate misbehaving children.
    (D) Children whose conduct is unacceptable are frequently sent to Koshari Kachina for lessons.

6. Click on the answer choice to which it in the passage refers.

   (A) doll
   (B) cottonwood tree
   (C) image of a particular kachina
   (D) small bit of the kachina

7. The word **motifs** in the passage is closest in meaning to

   (A) symbols
   (B) ceremonies
   (C) characters
   (D) foods

8. Click on the sentence in paragraph 3 that describes the function of the masks worn in ceremonies.

9. Which of the following is closest in meaning to intricate in the passage?

   (A) carved
   (B) detailed
   (C) wooden
   (D) colored

10. The decorations of kachina dolls mentioned in the passage do NOT include

    (A) baskets
    (B) leaves
    (C) incised symbols
    (D) painting

11. Which of the following can be inferred about the first kachina dolls?

    (A) Most were used to teach children.
    (B) They were not given to women.
    (C) They did not have a place of honor in the home.
    (D) Historians disagree over their use.

12. The passage does NOT provide information to answer which of the following questions?

    (A) What kind of wood is used in making kachina dolls?
    (B) What colors are used in painting kachina dolls?
    (C) During what time of year do the kachina live with the villages?
    (D) Where do the kachina live when they are not with the villages?

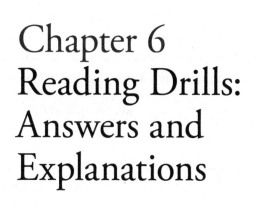

Chapter 6
Reading Drills:
Answers and
Explanations

READING DRILL #1 ANSWERS

1. **C** The beginning of paragraph 2 states, "*Commedia dell'arte*, unlike the literary comedy of the Renaissance, did not require written scripts." Therefore, the answer is (C).

2. **D** This is a Vocabulary in Context question, so work from context. The sentence surrounding "broad" states, "The humor was very broad—subtlety was a hallmark of many artistic achievements of the period, but not the *commedia dell'arte*." If subtlety is not a hallmark of *commedia dell'arte*, then this form of humor must be exaggerated, which is answer choice (D).

3. Role

   This is a Reference question, and the highlighted pronoun is not the subject of a verb. Therefore, you should test the noun immediately before the highlighted noun that agrees in number. In this case, it makes sense to say that performers "portrayed" a "role."

4. **C** Paragraph 2 states, "They also poked fun at the different regions of Italy by speaking in overdone accents." Therefore, the answer is (C).

5. **B** Paragraph 4 states, "Most actors kept notebooks, *zibaldone*, in which they noted down monologues, dialogues, and tag lines that their characters regularly rehearsed with." Therefore, the answer is (B).

6. **D** Paragraph 4 states, The plays they performed were improvised, but actors still needed a basic set of routine scenes and situations that could be altered in unexpected ways from one performance to another." Therefore, the answer is (D).

7. **C** This is another Vocabulary in Context question, so work from context. We are looking for what the *commedia dell'arte* became, and the sentence explains, " What had been a fresh and interesting method of improvisation at the end of the Renaissance turned stale by the end of the eighteenth century." If the *commedia dell'arte* changed from being fresh and interesting, we can most logically conclude that the genre had become boring or dull. Therefore, the answer is (C).

8. **A** Here is yet another Vocabulary in Context question, so work from context. "Progressively" describes the shift away from *commedia dell'arte*. More about that shift is described in the sentence, "As *commedia dell'arte* progressively became an institutionalized form of theater, improvisation itself began to seem old-fashioned." Since the shift is described as occurring as another phenomenon occurred, we can most logically conclude that it was gradual. Therefore, the answer is (A).

9. **B** This is an EXCEPT/LEAST/NOT question, so look for the answer choice that the passage does not support. Paragraph 5 states that audiences disliked "plotlines for not flowing believably and lacking a clear message." Therefore, this answer choice contradicts the passage and is the exception we want, and the answer is (B).

10. **C**   The last sentence of the passage states, "As a result, the *commedia dell'arte* was transformed. It evolved from presenting improvised performances of stereotyped characters toward following a script. The resulting performances both relied less on character types and expressed a clear moral lesson." Therefore, the answer is (C).

11.   Sixth sentence: **Audiences had tired of jokes in questionable taste, and they faulted the plotlines for not flowing believably and lacking a clear message.**

Be careful. There are sentences in the paragraph that mention conservatism but do not describe its specific aspects. The answer is the sixth sentence, "Audiences had tired of jokes in questionable taste, and they faulted the plotlines for not flowing believably and lacking a clear message."

12. **A**   The highlighted word indicates how the influence of *commedia dell'arte* relates to theater genres in other countries. If you're not sure that "detected" means "seen" or "recognized," use the process of elimination. You can't really "perform" or "translate" an influence, so you can eliminate (B) and (C) and guess. The answer is (A).

13.
   • Actors used exaggerated gestures, accents, and masks to give comic performances of stock characters.

   • The *commedia dell'arte*'s origin in street theater produced its emphasis on improvised performances.

   • *Commedia dell'arte* was forced to evolve when its vulgarity and lack of clear storylines lost favor with audiences.

The summary sentence is "The *commedia dell'arte* was a form of Italian theater that rose and fell in popularity between the sixteenth and eighteenth centuries" so we are looking for three ideas that will support this summary. "Actors used exaggerated gestures, accents, and masks to give comic performances of stock characters" should be included in the summary because this sentence is a definition of *commedia dell'arte*. "Similar kinds of improvised comic theater were developing in other European countries during the same period" should not be included in the summary because it is off-topic from the main idea, which is referencing Italian theater only. "'Comedy of artists' is not the best translation of *commedia dell'arte*" should not be included in the summary because it is an interesting fact but off-topic. "The *commedia dell'arte*'s origin in street theater produced its emphasis on improvised performances" should be included in the summary because this sentence gives us the origin of *commedia dell'arte*. The origin is important to note when talking about the rise and fall of the theater. *Commedia dell'arte* was forced to evolve when its vulgarity and lack of clear storylines lost favor with audiences" should be included in the summary because because this sentence gives us the evolution of *commedia dell'arte*. The evolution is important to note when talking about the rise and fall of the theater. "An unmarked mask was used to help actors practice their characters" should not be included in the summary because it is an interesting fact but off-topic.

READING DRILL #2 ANSWERS

1. **B**   This is a Vocabulary in Context question, so work from context. The word *oriented* describes the arrangement in which the long sides of buildings faced east and west. That means that it must refer to the layout of the workrooms. The answer is (B).

2. **A**   This is a Vocabulary in Context question, so work from context. The passage states, "most colonial Americans had to begin and end their day's activities with the sun," so the topic here is the amount of time that sunlight is available. The answer is (A).

3. **C**   This is a Vocabulary in Context question, so work from context. The sentence states, "Unfortunately, beeswax for candles was too dear for most households to afford for daily use," which indicates that most people could not spare the money to pay for beeswax. That means that beeswax must have been expensive. The answer is (C).

4. **D**   This is a reference question, and the pronoun is the subject of a sentence. Try substituting the subject of the previous sentence, and see whether the result makes sense. In this case, "the women of a household" clearly are the people who are dipping wicks in tallow to make candles. Therefore, the answer is (D).

5. **A**   The characteristics of tallow candles are described in paragraph 3, which states that "tallow candles were the least costly night lighting available to the average family." The paragraph also says that tallow candles "burned unevenly," "emitted a strong, unpleasant odor," and "produced almost as much smoke as light." That means that (B), (C), and (D) all contradict the passage. Therefore, the answer is (A).

6. **D**   This is a Reference question, and the pronoun is not the subject of the sentence. Start by substituting the previous noun that agrees, and see whether the sentence makes sense. In this case, the previous noun available as an answer choice is "stored candles," which are what the sentence describes as becoming unusable if exposed to heat. Therefore, the answer is (D).

7.   Tallow

   You're looking for the term that the passage defines. Remember to watch for common definition structures. In this case, the word "tallow" is followed by a noun phrase ("the fat that melted...") that explains what it is, so the answer is "tallow."

8. **C**   This is the eighth question, so its answer should come from near the end of the passage. A sentence in paragraph 5 states, "Fifteen pounds of bayberries were required to produce just one pound of wax, so bayberry wax was more expensive than tallow...." Be careful when evaluating the answer choices. Choice (A) is not supported by the passage, because we don't know how difficult it was for the colonists to discover bayberries. Choice (B) contradicts paragraph 4, which says that bayberries could be processed "as easily as tallow." Choice (D) is not supported by the passage, because we don't know whether the fragrance of the candles affected their cost. Therefore, the answer is (C).

9. **C** This is a Purpose question, so look for what the colonial records tell us about candles as sources of lighting, the main idea. The passage states, "Records from the period indicate that bayberry candles eventually nearly equaled tallow candles in popularity." What that tells us is how many colonists used bayberry candles, and therefore, the answer is (C).

10. You should insert it after the advantages of bayberries are listed, which is the third insertion point.

The sentence you are asked to insert into the passage refers back to "these advantages" and is related to bayberries. That means that you should insert it after the advantages of bayberries are listed, which is the third insertion point. The fourth insertion point may seem logical also, but the popularity of bayberry candles does not give an advantage that would make the candles worth the extra cost.

11. **C** Paragraph 5 does give high cost as a disadvantage of bayberries. But most of the passage discusses why they were easy to process, burned well, and became popular. These all indicate the usefulness of bayberries for candle making and, therefore, the answer is (C).

12. **A** This is a Vocabulary in Context question, so work from context. The sentence states, "The yield in finished candles was small, like that of beeswax (even if bayberry wax was as easy to process as tallow). Fifteen pounds of bayberries were required to produce just one pound of wax, so bayberry wax was more expensive than tallow." Because the sentences refer to the production involved in finished candles, the "yield" is "how many candles could be produced." Therefore, the answer is (A).

13.
- The most common candles were made of tallow, an animal fat that gave poor light.

- Candles made of bayberry wax had many advantages that made them popular despite their expense.
- Candle wicks burned slowly and needed constant attention.

The summary sentence is, "The candles colonists relied on to provide artificial light presented many difficulties" so we are looking for three ideas that will support this summary. "The most common candles were made of tallow, an animal fat that gave poor light" should be included in the summary because it describes one of the difficulties, poor light. "Candle makers were busy and often saw their productivity fall in winter" should not be included in the summary because it is off-topic from the main idea, which is referencing candles, not the candle makers. "Candles made of bayberry wax had many advantages that made them popular despite their expense" should be included in the summary because, though they had many advantages, their expense is a difficulty. "Beeswax was a material that produced candles with a pleasant fragrance" should not be included in the summary because it is a positive result, rather than a difficulty. "It took the colonists many years before they discovered how to extract wax from bayberries" should not be included in the summary because it is an interesting fact, but not essential to the main idea of the passage. "Candle wicks burned slowly and needed constant attention" should be included in the summary because two of the difficulties of candles are that they "burned slowly" and "needed constant attention."

READING DRILL #3 ANSWERS

1.   **D**   The passage discusses Paul MacLean's triune brain hypothesis throughout. Therefore, the answer is (D).

2.   **B**   The next several sentences make it clear that MacLean "refers to each body as a separate brain," "implying that the triune brain hypothesis expresses his belief. Therefore, the answer is (B).

3.   R-Complex

"It" refers to what "contains the programs responsible for hunting, homing, mating, establishing territory, and fighting." As the part of the brain under discussion here, the R-Complex is the best answer.

4.   **B**   Paragraph 4 states, "After destruction of part of the limbic system, young mammals stop playing...." Thus, it follows that the limbic system is a site of the sense of play. Therefore, the answer is (B).

5.   **C**   Paragraph 4 states, "The cortex seems to control the memorization and problem-solving useful to aid the two older bodies in the struggle for survival." If the other two formulations are older, then it follows that the cortex must be the newest. Therefore, the answer is (C).

6.   **A**   The passage states, "The prefrontal areas of the cortex are the most highly developed." Therefore, the answer is (A).

7.   MacLean considers the cortex like a computer that can look into the future and anticipate the consequences of actions.

We're looking here for a metaphor, so we need to find a direct comparison between a part of the brain and something else. The sentence that does this is, "MacLean considers the cortex like a computer that can look into the future and anticipate the consequences of actions."

8.   **D**   The passage states, "According to triune brain theory, the development of the prefrontal fibers was the most auspicious turn of events in the history of biology." It makes sense to state that a biological development was an unexpected change of circumstances. Therefore, the answer is (D).

9.   **A**   This is a Vocabulary in Context question, so work from context. The passage quotes Paul MacLean as saying, in MacLean's words, "It is this new development that makes possible the insight required to plan for the needs of others as well as the self and to use our knowledge to alleviate suffering everywhere." Even if you do not know that alleviate means "lessen," you can conclude that planning for the needs of others would involve lessening suffering. The answer is (A).

10.   This sentence gives more detail about the ability to "look into the future and anticipate the conse-quences of actions" which MacLean mentions in the sentence before the second square.

The sentence you are asked to insert into the passage gives more detail about the ability to "look into the future and anticipate the consequences of actions" that MacLean mentions in the sentence before the second square.

11.   **B**   The passage states that MacLean has studied the R-Complex by "experimenting with the R-com-plex in animals such as squirrel monkeys and turkeys." Therefore, the answer is (B).

12.   **A**   The highlighted sentence in the passage is, "That the brain has distinct regions at which different activities are centered is well accepted, although it is now known that few functions are performed exclusively by a single section of the brain." In other words, "any given function can be performed by several regions of the brain, but tends to be concentrated in one special area" so the answer is choice (A).

13.   •   The cortex is the part of the brain humans share with higher mammals, their closest modern-day relatives.

•   The R-complex and the limbic system are parts of the brain inherited from ancient ancestors.

•   The prefrontal areas of the cortex may be the site of the self-awareness and generosity we think of as characteristically human.

The summary sentence is "Researcher Paul McLean has developed a theory of the human brain called the triune brain hypothesis" so we are looking for three ideas that will support this sum-mary. "McLean works with several types of animals to find similarities between their brains and ours" should not be included in the summary because it is an interesting fact but is not essential to the main idea. "Scientists study brain function by measuring electrical activity while subjects speak, read, and write" should not be included in the summary because it is an interesting fact but is not essential to the main idea. "The cortex is the part of the brain humans share with higher mammals, their closest modern-day relatives" should be included in the summary because it re-lates to McLean's theory. "The R-complex and the limbic system are parts of the brain inherited from ancient ancestors" should be included in the summary because it relates to McLean's theory. "McLean's theory is highly controversial, though no specific component of it has been disproved" should not be included in the summary because it is an interesting fact but is not essential to the main idea. "The prefrontal areas of the cortex may be the site of the self-awareness and generosity we think of as characteristically human" should be included in the summary because it relates to McLean's theory.

READING DRILL #4 ANSWERS

1. **A** The passage discusses how Eakins combined artistic and medical training to form a distinctive realistic style. Therefore the answer is (A).

2. Painting

    The highlighted word refers to what "shocked many of Eakins's contemporaries." From context, we know that what was shocking was *The Gross Clinic*, which showed blood in the operating room. "Painting" is the only highlighted word noun phrase that refers to *The Gross Clinic*, so it is the best answer.

3. **D** The sixth sentence in the second paragraph states, "The school's dissecting rooms were not normal places for young artists to visit…" implying that it was not common for artists to take classes at a medical school. Also keep in mind that the third paragraph mentions that "paintings from battles had often portrayed the wounded as bleeding" which directly contradicts choice (C). Therefore, the answer is (D).

4. **C** The passage states, "But Eakins's technique also lent his subjects an air of thoughtfulness. By refusing to idealize them, he showed them to be people with complex personalities. These portraits were at the opposite extreme from the creations of fashionable painters of the day." Combined, these sentences indicate that what made Eakins's paintings different from those of fashionable painters was the thoughtfulness he showed in them. Therefore, the answer is (C).

5. **A** Paragraph 4 states, "Understanding bone and muscle structure allowed him to create two-dimensional paintings in which people seem to exist with depth, weight, and emotion." Therefore, the answer is (A).

6. **B** This is a Vocabulary in Context question, so work from context. The passage states, "Eakins's paintings, as well as his training, showed his unusual commitment to realism. When he wanted to attract attention with a major picture, he painted a surgical operation: *The Gross Clinic*. This painting showed scientists routinely, if bloodily, at work, and it shocked many of Eakins's contemporaries." *The Gross Clinic* is discussed as a major picture in terms of how well it attracts attention. Therefore, the answer is (B).

7. **B** Routine means "following established practice." Therefore, the answer is (B).

8. **C** Contemporaries are people who live at the same time in history. Therefore, the answer is (C).

9. **B** When a question asks what comes after the passage, remember to look for a new topic introduced in the last sentence. The passage has already discussed Eakins and his achievements, so the logical way for the passage to continue would be with the "anti-naturalistic movements in Modern art" that are mentioned for the first time at the end. Therefore, the answer is (B).

10. "The moments he chose to depict were frequently those at which muscles were most contracted or extended, in order to capture peaks of tension."

You're looking for the sentence that describes Eakins's goals for his portraits; if you skimmed and mapped well, you should know that this information is likely to be found in the second half of the passage. Of the bold-faced sentences, ("The school's dissecting rooms...") describes why Eakins studied anatomy but not why he painted people. The second ("When he wanted...") and third ("Paintings from battles...") describe a painting that was designed to get attention, but not to a portrait. Therefore, only the fourth sentence, which explains that Eakins aimed to "capture peaks of tension," describes what Eakins was trying to do in his paintings of athletes.

11. **C** The main topic of the passage is why Eakins is considered a great artist. And the main topic of paragraph 3 is that *The Gross Clinic*, although "today considered a masterpiece," showed blood in a way that "had no place in art that depicted everyday life." In this context, the information that the painting was sold for a small sum indicates that it was not considered valuable by buyers, and the information that it was purchased by a medical school indicates that it was not considered valuable by art collectors. Therefore, the answer is (C).

12. **A** This is a Detail question that asks for an exception. Look at the section on portrait paintings, and eliminate answers that don't fit. From paragraph 5, you can eliminate (D) ("In these paintings, the bone and muscle structures beneath the skin were suggested with subtle variations of paint color and texture"), (B) ("He required his models to sit for a long time, which made it difficult for them to retain their formal posture."), and (C) ("By refusing to idealize them, he showed them to be people with complex personalities"). Therefore, the answer that remains is (A).

13.
- He painted very realistically, without making people's features look artificially happy.

- He used paint effects to suggest underlying body structures.

- He studied anatomy as well as taking art training.

The summary sentence is "Thomas Eakins developed a unique style of painting based on his training and approach to his subjects" so we are looking for three ideas that will support this summary. "He painted very realistically, without making people's features look artificially happy" should be included in the summary because this sentence describes his unique style of painting. "One of Eakins's most famous paintings was initially refused exhibition" should not be included in the summary because it is an interesting fact but is not essential to the main idea "He took photographs in addition to painting" should not be included in the summary because the main idea focuses on his painting, not his photographs. "He used paint effects to suggest underlying body structures" should be included in the summary because this sentence describes his unique style of painting. "He studied anatomy as well as taking art training" should be included in the summary because this sentence describes the way in which his training, a word mentioned in the main idea, lead to his unique style. "He spent most of his life painting scenes from his native Philadelphia" should not be included in the summary because it is an interesting fact but is not essential to the main idea.

READING DRILL #5 ANSWERS

1. **C** The answer to a Main Idea question needs to apply to the entire passage. Here, the first paragraph describes how flax is obtained from the plant, the second paragraph outlines some of the history of flax use, and the third discusses how flax is used today. Therefore, the answer is (C).

2. **C** This is a Vocabulary in Context question, so work from context. The word "brittle" goes along with the description of the pith of the plant as "woody," and the fibers around it are later described as "inflexible," so the best indication is that the highlighted word means something like "stiff." Therefore, the answer is (C).

3. **A** When asked for the main idea of a paragraph, remember that the first sentence usually introduces the topic clearly, though you will need to supplement it with the rest of the information in the paragraph. The first sentence of paragraph 2 mentions the versatility of linen, and the rest of the sentences mention different societies and time periods in which linen was used. Therefore, the answer is (A).

4. **C** This is a Vocabulary in Context question, so work from context. The highlighted is part of an explanation that "farmers must cultivate flax plants in 'close stands,' clustering them tightly so that the stems do not form branches as the plants grow." Since the word refers to how flax is planted "tightly" in "close stands," it makes sense to conclude that it means something like "grouping." Therefore, the answer is (C).

5. **B** The Detail you're asked about here comes from paragraph 2. You want to find the goal of planting in "close stands," so look for words that indicate reasons or objectives: "In order to produce fibers that are long enough to spin into yarn, farmers must cultivate flax plants in 'close stands,' clustering them tightly so that the stems do not form branches as the plants grow." Since "close stands" produce long fibers that don't branch, they must prevent short, branched fibers. The answer is (B).

6. **D** This is another Detail question answered in paragraph 2: "The raw fibers are too inflexible to use in textiles, and they stick to other parts of the plant. So before removal from the stems they must be softened. Flax farmers let the stems sit in a warm, moist environment to allow fermenting bacteria to digest them partially." The purpose of putting fibers into a warm, moist environment is to soften them through bacteria. Therefore, the answer is (D).

7. **A** This is a Reference question in which the highlighted pronoun is not the subject of a verb. Therefore, try the closest previous noun that agrees in number and gender. In this case, "fibers" makes sense as what are digested by bacteria. Therefore, the answer is (A).

8. **B** The passage mentions that, "though flax fibers are less flexible than cotton fibers, they are longer and stronger overall." In other words, linen lasts longer (resists decay) and is stronger (durable) than cotton. Therefore, the answer is (B).

9.   flax fibers

This is a Reference question, so work from context. The highlighted pronoun is the subject of a verb, so test the closest previous subject that agrees in number and gender. In this case, "flax fibers" makes sense as the longer and stronger fiber in the comparison. Therefore, the answer is flax fibers.

10.   **B**   This is a Detail question with an EXCEPT answer choice format, so start by checking the answer that seems most likely to be inaccurate. The part of the passage we've just worked with for the last few questions states, "Mechanical looms developed in the sixteenth century speeded the weaving of cotton, but they pulled yarns too roughly to be used with delicate linen. Creasing repeatedly along the same line will also eventually cause cracks to appear in linen. Still, though flax fibers are less flexible than cotton fibers, they are longer and stronger overall. Since finely woven linen is so smooth and lustrous, it is one of the most valuable textiles." Both the statement that linen yarn cannot be pulled hard, and the statement that linen is less flexible than cotton indicate that flexibility is not an advantage that linen has. Therefore, the answer is (B).

11.   creasing repeatedly

This is a Detail question, so use a lead word in the question rather than just reading around the answer choices first. Your looking for how linen fabric can be damaged, which is discussed in paragraph 3: "Creasing repeatedly along the same line will also eventually cause cracks to appear in linen." Therefore, the answer is creasing repeatedly.

12.   You should insert the sentence at the second insertion point.

Treat Sentence Insertion questions like Detail questions: look for a lead word or trigger word in the sentence, then find corresponding ideas in the passage. We need information about looms and adaptability, since "nevertheless" along with "they did not always adapt" indicates a contrast. Test the sentence between the one about adaptability and the one about looms: "Linen fibers adapted readily to incorporation into garments, sailcloth, writing paper, and insulation. Nevertheless, they did not always adapt to advances in the designs of looms themselves. Mechanical looms developed in the sixteenth century speeded the weaving of cotton, but they pulled yarns too roughly to be used with delicate linen." The flow is logical, so this is the best insertion point.

13.
- When properly processed, linen fibers are strong and conduct heat well.

- The fibers are not visible when the flax plant is viewed from the outside.

- Flax plants must be specially cultivated and softened before the fibers can be removed and processed for use.

The summary sentence is "Linen cloth made from flax fibers requires effort to produce but has many advantages" so we are looking for three ideas that will support this summary. "As linen has become more popular, Ireland is competing with other sources of linen for customers" should not be included in the summary because the main idea is the production of linen, not the countries who are competing for customers. "The Egyptians associated linen with royalty and the priesthood" should not be included in the summary because this statement does not refer to the production of linen, which is the main idea. "When properly processed, linen fibers are strong and conduct heat well" should be included in the summary because this sentence references the production of linen. "The fibers are not visible when the flax plant is viewed from the outside" should be included in the summary because this sentence relates to the main idea: linen cloth that is made from flax fibers requires effort to produce. "Flax plants must be specially cultivated and softened before the fibers can be removed and processed for use" should be included in the summary because this sentence relates to the main idea, linen cloth that is made from flax fibers requires effort to produce. "More sensitive machines used in processing have made it easier to mass-produce linen for modern consumers" should not be included in the summary because this sentence focuses on the machinery used, instead of the linen itself.

READING DRILL #6 ANSWERS

1. **D**   Paragraph 1 introduces moths as being diverse and interesting. Paragraph 2 describes how various types of adult moths defend themselves, and paragraph 3 describes the defenses of moth larvae and pupae. Since the only topic that recurs throughout the passage is the survival strategies that moths employ, the answer is (D).

2. **C**   This is a Vocabulary in Context question, so work from context. The sentence that contains the highlighted word uses "while" to contrast "butterflies have a more eminent place in the popular imagination" with "moths are greater in total numbers and in number of species." That means that "eminent" must match up with "great" somehow. Therefore, the answer is (C)

3. **A**   Paragraph 1 states, "most hunt, mate, and migrate at night," indicating only some moths are active during the day. Note that you need not understand the word "diurnal" to figure this out. Therefore, the answer is (A).

4. **B**   Paragraph 2 states that some moths survive by "imitating either a stick or a leaf to blend in with the environment." If imitating sticks or leaves allows them to "blend in with the environment," it must make them difficult to see. Therefore, the answer is (B).

5. Shared

   This is a Vocabulary in Context question, so work from context. The highlighted word describes the silk tent, and we know that "hundreds or thousands" of pupae can be housed there. The best indication is that the tent is a "group" tent, and the only bold-faced word with that meaning is "shared." The answer is shared.

6.   **B**   The passage states that some moths have "eye-shaped markings that make them look threatening." Therefore, the answer is (B).

7.   **B**   This is a Vocabulary in Context question, so work from context. If "pose" is what moths can or cannot do with threats toward predators, it must have a general meaning such as "do." Of the answer choices, "present" is the closest. Therefore, the answer is (B).

8.   **B**   Paragraph 2 says of Eastern tent caterpillars, "If threatened, they have a shared strategy for frightening predators: they thrash about, thus shaking the tent." Therefore, the answer is (B).

9.   **D**   This is a Vocabulary in Context question, so work from context. "Harboring" is something that puts moth pupae "out of sight" and provides "coverage" under soil or water. Therefore, it seems to involve hiding the larvae, and the answer is (D).

10.   **C**   This is a Detail question answered near the end of the passage: "At this phase, a developing moth is least mobile and most vulnerable to attack." Therefore, the answer is (C).

11.   **B**   This one requires a little work, but by this point, you should be familiar enough with the passage to find the answer quickly. Paragraph 3 says of adult moths, "Such actual counterattacks as moths are capable of making are usually chemical. One species spits acid into its enemy's eyes." Paragraph 5 says of Eastern tent caterpillars, "If this strategy fails, the Eastern tent caterpillars emit a mixture of noxious chemicals." Therefore, the answer is (B).

12.   **C**   The highlighted sentence in the passage is, "The moths' disguise only needs to be passable enough to fool forest animals, whose vision generally has low resolution power; however, many actually look amazingly realistic even close up." In other words, a moth does not necessarily need to camouflage itself so impressively because its predators have poor eyesight.

13.   The summary sentence is "Moths have several strategies that they use to survive, despite their inability to fight back well against predators" so we are looking for three ideas that will support this summary.

   - "Adult moths can fly, so they can make themselves less identifiable through mimicry or surprise a predator with chemicals"

   - "As long as caterpillars can distract predators temporarily, they usually have time to crawl to safety"

   - "Pupae cannot move, so they remain out of sight or rely on caterpillars to ward off predators"

"Adult moths can fly, so they can make themselves less identifiable through mimicry or surprise a predator with chemicals" should be included in the summary because this is a strategy moths use to survive, which is the main idea. "As long as caterpillars can distract predators temporarily, they usually have time to crawl to safety" should be included in the summary because this is a strategy moths use to survive, which is the main idea. "Moths perform useful functions, so it is worth it for humans to protect them from harm" should not be included in the summary because this is a wishful statement, not the main idea, that moths have several strategies to protect themselves. "Markings that are frightening to predators are often beautiful to humans who study moths" should not be included in the summary because, while this is an interesting point, it is not essential to the main idea. "Pupae cannot move, so they remain out of sight or rely on caterpillars to ward off predators" should be included in the summary because this is a strategy moths use to survive, which is the main idea. "Predators avoid poisonous insects, so moths that are poisonous find it easier to survive" should not be included in the summary because this idea is not in the passage.

READING DRILL #7 ANSWERS

1. **A** Paragraphs 1 and 2 introduce Julia Morgan as an architect and detail her education. Paragraph 3 explains Morgan's reclusive nature on construction sites. Paragraph 4 discusses Morgan's focus on interior spaces in her work and Paragraph 5 shows the importance of Morgan in the field of architecture. The whole essay is devoted to Julia Morgan's career as an architect so the answer is (A).

2. **A** This is a Vocabulary in Context question, so work from context. The word *shunned* is used to describe one way Morgan was able to "avoid celebrity" so the answer is (A).

3. **C** This is a Detail question answered in the third paragraph. The passage states that "When she retired, she ordered all of her papers burned believing that an architect should be like the usually anonymous medieval master builders who created Europe's vast monasteries, cathedrals, and castle." Therefore the answer is (C).

4. **C** This is a Vocabulary in Context question, so work from context. The next sentence states that Morgan's buildings are "elegant testimony to her brilliant architectural vision." Therefore the answer is (C).

5. **C** This one is a little tougher than the first four questions on the passage. Paragraph 3 states that Morgan "focus on and cater to the individual" so eliminate (A). Paragraph 4 claims that Morgan was a creator of "great buildings nobly planned" so we can eliminate (B). Paragraph 2 shows that Morgan "avoided celebrity" so cross off (D). Using the Process of Elimination, the answer is (C).

6. Her house designs demonstrated respect for the everyday needs of the residents.

   This sentence claims that Morgan held an attitude of respect for the people who lived in houses that she built.

7. **C** This is a Vocabulary in Context question, so work from context. The passage states that Morgan "focused" on the individual and "strove to build structures that were practical to live and work in." These words are closest in meaning to the word "goal." Therefore the answer is (C).

8. **D** The passage only mentions one collaboration so we cannot infer that she worked with many architects; eliminate choice (A). The text never mentions money so it cannot be choice (B). Paragraph 3 states that Morgan was not interested in developing her own unique style so eliminate (C). Paragraph 3 claims that "Morgan strove to build structures that were practical to live and work in" so we know that she created spaces that were useful. Therefore the answer is (D).

9. **C** Steilberg's comment that Morgan's "object was first of all to build a home" is used to support the claim that "Morgan strove to build structures that were practical to live and work in." Therefore the answer is (C).

10. **D** This is a Detail question answered in the fourth paragraph. The passage states that Morgan was "a rare architect with little ego" which indicates that other architects probably had a large ego. Therefore the answer is (D).

11. **C** This is a Detail question answered at the end of the passage. The passage states that Morgan was a "designer of simple dwellings and stately homes." Therefore the answer is (C).

12. **B** The highlighted sentence is "With its pleasing straightforwardness and lack of waste, Morgan's style warrants more attention than it sometimes receives in the world of contemporary architecture, which values extravagance." In other words, Julia Morgan had a style that should get more attention.

13. **C** Paragraph 2 argues that "complications resulting from surgery on her inner ear left her face asymmetrical" and that Morgan's "physical awkwardness only encouraged her innate reclusive tendencies and pushed her further from the public eye." Therefore the answer is (C).

READING DRILL #8 ANSWERS

1. **B** Paragraph 1 introduces the concept of glassmaking in the United States. Paragraphs 2 and 3 discuss the growth of glassmaking in the colonies. Paragraph 4 mentions other types of glassmaking that were popular in the United States during the period. Therefore the answer is (B).

2. **A** This is a Detail question found in the second paragraph which begins by stating that "There were problems on the demand side also" and then mentions that "American glass was thought to be practical but somewhat crude." Therefore the answer is (A).

3. **C** This is a Vocabulary in Context question, so work from context. The passage states that affluent Americans could "afford expensive glass items." Therefore the answer is (C).

4. **A** This is a Vocabulary in Context question, so work from context. "Perception" refers to the fact that "American glass was thought to be practical but somewhat crude." "Thought" is closest in meaning to impression. Therefore the answer is (A).

5. **C** This is a Vocabulary in Context question, so work from context. The third paragraph discusses several new developments that came about in the late nineteenth century following in time after German immigrants brought lead crystal to Pennsylvania. Therefore the answer is (C).

6. **D** This is a Vocabulary in Context question, so work from context. The final paragraph refers to two properties of glass: color and clarity. These are characteristics so (D) is the answer.

7. **B** This is a Detail question found in the third paragraph which states that new "tools produced many of the effects of old hand-cutting, but they required less skill." Therefore the answer is (B).

8. **D** This is a Detail question found in the last paragraph which states that natural glass was "slightly blue" which makes (D) the credited response.

9. **C** This is a Detail question found in the last paragraph. The second sentence claims that milk glass "was often pressed into patterns rather than cut" which answers the question "How could patterns be added to glasswares without cutting?" Therefore (C) is the answer.

10. **D** The popularity of American glass is discussed in the third paragraph. The paragraph mentions that America had an abundance of sand for use in glassmaking, new technology that advanced glassmaking in important ways, and that wealthy consumers caused the demand to increase. The passage does not mention a lack of competition, therefore the answer is (D).

11. Paragraph 2

    The question asks for the paragraph which shows the introduction of glass cutting and paragraph 2 states that "Mixing in small amounts of lead made the glass clear and soft enough to be cut into patterns that reflected light attractively, a technique long associated with the skilled craftsmen of the European cities of Venice and Prague."

12. **C** The highlighted sentence is The innovation of American manufacturers was to treat it as a material with pleasing properties of its own instead, freeing their imaginations to mold it into new shapes and designs. In other words, American glassmakers created products with milk glass that were not imitations of porcelain.

13. The summary sentence is "**American glassmaking developed slowly but eventually became the best in the world**," so we are looking for three ideas that will support this summary.

    - "America's high-quality sand and advances in technology allowed glassmaking to improve as demand increased"

    - "Glassmakers developed types of products, ranging from milk glass to clear colored glass, that were the finest of their kind"

    - "A combination of British policy and prejudice among potential local buyers discouraged the development of glassmaking in the colonies"

"America's high-quality sand and advances in technology allowed glassmaking to improve as demand increased" should be included because these advances are part of the main idea. "Some people prefer glass made with traditional furnaces and tools, despite difficulties of quality control" should not be included because it is not stated in the passage. "Glassmakers developed types of products, ranging from milk glass to clear colored glass, that were the finest of their kind" should be included because the high quality of American glass is part of the main idea. "Natural glass is not perfectly clear because of impurities in the sand from which it is made" should not be included because it does not support the main idea about the development of glassmaking in the United States. "A combination of British policy and prejudice among potential local buyers discouraged the development of glassmaking in the colonies" should be included because it is one of the reasons that glassmaking developed slowly. "The most advanced centers of glass production at the time were Venice and Prague" should not be included because it does not support the main idea about the development of glassmaking in the United States.

READING DRILL #9 ANSWERS

1. **D** Paragraph 1 introduces the idea of increasing financial and energy costs associated with transportation. Paragraphs 2 through 4 discuss changes in transportation of goods to a system that is more expensive and uses more energy than alternatives. Paragraphs 5 and 6 argue that similar economical and energy-use problems also occur in new systems of public transportation.

2. **A** This Detail question is found in the second paragraph. The passage states that "Transporting a ton of goods by truck consumes four times as much energy as transporting the same ton by train over the same distance. Transporting a ton of goods by truck consumes four times as much energy as transporting the same ton by train over the same distance." Therefore the answer is (A).

3. **C** This is a Vocabulary in Context question, so work from context. The passage is comparing energy use in truck versus train transportation. Therefore the answer is (C).

4. **D** This Detail question is found in the fourth paragraph. There the passage states that commuters "place a greater strain not only on the economy, but also on the environment. The emissions from millions of automobiles send a flood of pollutants into the air." Therefore the answer is (D).

5. **B** This Detail question is found in the fourth paragraph which states that people use more nonrenewable resources because they "live farther away from their place of work." Therefore the answer is (B).

6. **D** This Detail question is found in the fourth paragraph. The highlighted word is in a sentence about the commute of city-dwellers that says "The average commute now takes more than forty-five minutes, more than it took a century ago when city-dwellers lived near the jobs they commuted to and could take public transportation such as trolley cars." Therefore the answer is (D).

7. **C** The fourth paragraph states that "the emissions from millions of automobiles send a flood of pollutants into the air above major industrial areas and cause health problems." Therefore the answer is (C).

8. **A** The passage states that "the average American now spends more per year on an automobile than on food" which indicates that Americans spend a significant amount on transportation. The answer is (A).

9. **A** This is a Vocabulary in Context question, so work from context. The passage states that city space is devoted to automobile movement and storage and that cities are trying to "use valuable space more efficiently." Therefore the answer is (A).

10. **B** This is a Vocabulary in Context question, so work from context. The passage states that the resolutions are ways for cities who are "trying to use valuable space more efficiently." Therefore the answer is (B).

11. **B** The passage states that cities that "recognize that more than half of their downtown land area is devoted to the movement and storage of automobiles, are taking steps to improve public transportation in order to use valuable space more efficiently." The answer is (B).

12. **C** The final paragraph of the passage states that "Putting people and their destinations closer together does decrease the distances they must travel by car, but it increases the number of people using the same roads. In other words, traffic congestion rises, and travel times may not decrease significantly." Therefore the answer is (C).

13. The summary sentence is "**Increased use of the automobile for transportation has produced both advantages and disadvantages,**" so we are looking for three ideas that will support this summary.

   - "People prefer the freedom of traveling by car despite traffic congestion and high energy consumption"

   - "Delivering goods by truck requires more energy while making scheduling more flexible" should be used because it discusses a disadvantage of automobile transportation.

   - "Most freight used to be transported by train to large warehouses in a few key locations"

   "Public transportation options include not only light rail trains but also electric trolley cars" should not be used because it does not discuss advantages or disadvantages of automobile transportation. "People prefer the freedom of traveling by car despite traffic congestion and high energy consumption" should be used because it discusses a reason people use automobile transportation despite its disadvantages. "Research indicates that development planning can increase population densities while decreasing traffic congestion" should not be used because it does not discuss advantage or disadvantages of automobile transportation. "Delivering goods by truck requires more energy while making scheduling more flexible" should be used because it discusses a disadvantage of automobile transportation. "Most freight used to be transported by train to large warehouses in a few key locations" should be used because it discusses the increased use of automobile transportation. "Cities such as Portland have not created policies that strike a balance between saving resources and pleasing consumers" should not be used because it does not discuss advantage or disadvantages of automobile transportation.

READING DRILL #10 ANSWERS

1. **C** This is a Vocabulary in Context question, so work from context. Use the whole passage for context on this question since it is the first question on the passage. The entire passage discusses cowboys as interesting figures, and the last sentence refers to cowboys as having a "picturesque" and "romantic" life. These are closest to "interesting" so (C) is the answer.

2. **B** This is a detail question found in the second paragraph. The passage states that "Cowhands worked sunup to sundown and received lower wages than most factory workers" to show that cowboys made little money. Therefore the answer is (B).

3. **B** The second paragraph states that many cowboys "developed permanent squints from looking into the glaring sunlight" so the answer is (B).

4. **D** The second paragraph mentions the plains and there are no mentions of other land areas worked by cowboys in the passage. Therefore the answer is (D).

5. **A** This is a Vocabulary in Context question, so work from context. The passage mentions that cowboys had to protect themselves from "all the dust raised by the running of countless cattle" so there must have been many cattle creating dust. Therefore the answer is (A).

6. **D** The passage states that bandannas "served as a towel, a napkin, and a bandage." You can eliminate answers (A), (B), and (C) so the credited response is (D).

7. **C** The sentences surrounding the highlighted portion read "Cowhands sometimes wore leather trousers called chaps over regular overalls. They protected the legs from injury if a rider fell from a horse or had to ride through cactus, sagebrush, or other thorny plants." Since chaps protect the legs, the word "they" is referring to chaps and the answer is (C).

8. **C** The passage states that the trail boss had to have "good judge of character and [be] a good handler of various personalities." These characteristics are closest to "work with people" so the answer is (C).

9. **A** The passage states that cowboys had to ride horses during long drives with cattle but never mentions cowboys needing to make their own equipment. Therefore the answer is (A).

10. **B** The first paragraph states that "These *vaqueros*, the Spanish term for cowboy, invented almost all the tools of the cowhand's trade, from the distinctive hat and rope lariat to the special saddle." Therefore the answer is (B).

11. **D** The passage states that today, cowboys work in a truck "so the danger of injury is low and supplies are accessible" which indicates their job has been made easier. Therefore the answer is (D).

12. **B** The bolded sentence is "**A good cook was essential to a successful drive, as the morale of the men often depended on him, and he was called upon to play doctor, nurse, and even barber.**" In other words, the cook held many jobs and was an important part of a cattle drive.

13. The summary sentence is "The cowboy deserves his reputation for doing difficult work under harsh conditions," so we are looking for three ideas that will support this summary.

- "Cowboys required items of protective clothing to avoid the damaging effects of weather and desert plants"

- "Cowboys' work was so physically demanding that it damaged their legs and skin"

- "Long drives were conducted with a minimum of equipment and few workers to take care of the cowboys"

"Some words for cowboy equipment were adopted from the Spanish used by Mexican cowboys" should not be used because it does not address the hard work or conditions for cowboys. "Cowboys required items of protective clothing to avoid the damaging effects of weather and desert plants" should be used because it is about the gear required by cowboys to deal with the harsh conditions. "Cowboys' work was so physically demanding that it damaged their legs and skin" should be used because it discusses the hard work done by cowboys. "The trail boss was in charge of choosing both the route and the employees for a long drive" should not be used because it does not address the hard work or conditions for cowboys. "Long drives were conducted with a minimum of equipment and few workers to take care of the cowboys" should be used because it discusses the harsh conditions under which cowboys did work. "More people are interested in becoming cowhands now that modern equipment can be used" should not be used because it does not address the hard work or conditions for cowboys.

READING DRILL #11 ANSWERS

1. **A** This is a Vocabulary in Context question, so work from context. Use the whole passage for context on this question since it is the first question on the passage. The passage states that Angkor was the "center of civilization" so the answer is (A).

2. **D** The passage states that the ruins Angkor Wat had an "imposing scale" indicating that they are very large. Therefore the answer is (D).

3. **A** The author states that "the ruins of the temples of Angkor Wat are among the most impressive in the world" so there is a high level of respect given to the ruins and the answer is (A).

4. **D** The second paragraph states that "archaeologists are only beginning to ponder" the death of the Khmer empire. Therefore the answer is (D).

5. **A** The passage states that the ruins of "Angkor Wat indicate that the empire that created it was highly advanced and powerful." Therefore thriving means prosperous and the answer is (A).

6. **C** The second paragraph states that "Large-scale farming around Tonlé Sap was impossible without irrigation" so it could not have been naturally suited to agriculture. Therefore the answer is (C).

7. **B** The highlighted word is in the following text: "The temples and palaces of Angkor were constructed around a series of artificial reservoirs and canals, which were annually flooded to capacity by the Mekong River. Once filled, they were used to irrigate the surrounding rice paddies and farmland over the course of the year." The word "they" references something that was filled and the prior sentence states that artificial reservoirs and canals were filled with water. Therefore the answer is (B).

8. **A** The passage states that "the construction of hundreds of sandstone temples and palaces required an enormous amount of physical labor" indicating that the population growth was due to people moving into the city for work. Therefore the answer is (A).

9. **B** The passage states that "the demand for food skyrocketed so quickly it outstripped the ability of the irrigation system to satisfy it. Efforts by farmers to increase productivity of rice also over-worked the soil, leading to erosion and nutrient depletion." From this we can eliminate answers (A), (C), and (D) so the answer must be (B).

10. **D** The passage indicates that scientists and archaeologists have theories and speculation about what caused the decline of Khmer empire but there is no mention of a clear and definite reason. Therefore the answer is (D).

11. **C** The passages states that "the demand for food skyrocketed so quickly it outstripped the ability of the irrigation system to satisfy it." The high demand was too much for the irrigation system so (C), exceeded, is the answer.

12.   C   The passage states that "The popularity of [Theravada Buddhism] decreased the incentive to obey the higher classes without questioning. The labor to support massive public works projects became difficult to obtain." Therefore the answer is (C).

13.   The summary sentence is "**There are several factors that could explain the decline of the city of Angkor,**" so we are looking for three ideas that will support this summary.

    •   "The people of the countryside stopped giving labor and tribute to the Khmer rulers"

    •   "Excessive farming caused the soil and the irrigation system to deteriorate"

    •   "Invasions by neighboring societies weakened the political power of the Khmer Empire"

    "The city was not deserted suddenly but rather over a period of centuries" should not be used because it doesn't talk about a reason for the decline of Angkor. "The people of the countryside stopped giving labor and tribute to the Khmer rulers" should be used because it provides one reason for the decline of Angkor. "Excessive farming caused the soil and the irrigation system to deteriorate" should be used because it provides one reason for the decline of Angkor. "The invading Thai Empire destroyed everything in the city besides the Angkor Wat complex" should not be used because it doesn't talk about a reason for the decline of Angkor. "Invasions by neighboring societies weakened the political power of the Khmer Empire" should be used because it provides one reason for the decline of Angkor. "Researchers are still not sure how Khmer laborers could have produced the larger structures of the Angkor Wat complex" should not be used because it does not mention a reason for the decline of Angkor.

READING DRILL #12 ANSWERS

1.   A   The main point of the passage is to discuss the "key scientific discoveries" of Paracelsus. Therefore the answer is (A).

2.   D   This is a Vocabulary in Context question, so work from context. The passages states that Paracelsus made "key scientific discoveries" that had a "far-reaching impact" on medicine. This is closest in meaning to *important* so the answer is (D).

3.   D   The passage states that "By maintaining reference works in ancient Latin (or sometimes ancient Greek and Arabic), which most outsiders could not read, the Doctors of Physick prevented others from questioning their beliefs and treatments." Therefore the answer is (D).

4.   A   The passage states that "Early studies of human anatomy were seriously hampered by factors not directly related to the difficulty of understanding the structures of the body" and lists the inability to dissect as an example of this in the following sentence. Therefore the answer is (A).

5.   point-branding

The passage claims that "For patients with complaints about the mind rather than the body, point brandings were performed with heated needles."

6.   D   The passage states that some Doctors of Physick performed treatments that "when applied inappropriately, these treatments had no effect or actually worsened the condition of a patient." This indicates that not all patients were helped by treatments so the answer is (D).

7.   C   This is a Vocabulary in Context question, so work from context. The passage states that "understandably, many common people opted to get medicines from village apothecaries" rather than go to Doctors. Therefore the answer is (C).

8.   B   The passage states that "Paracelsus was a self-taught medicine man who took a practical approach to medicine, rather than following the traditions that had grown up around it." Therefore the answer is (B).

9.   C   The fourth paragraph states that "This violated the Hippocratic oath, in which the Doctor of Physick swore to guard his professional knowledge." Therefore the answer is (C).

10. B   The passage notes that "Given his record of, time after time, putting a higher priority on a straightforward understanding of medicine than on respect for tradition, it was no surprise when Paracelsus was ejected from the university in 1528. His philosophy, however, had begun to have its effect and could not be stopped." This indicates that Paracelsus was kicked out or "removed" from the university. Therefore (B) is the credited response.

11. C   The last sentence of the passage states that "this was just the beginning of the far-reaching impact Paracelsus had on Western medicine." We would expect the next paragraph to continue talking about other ways Paracelsus impacted medicine. Therefore (C) is the answer.

12. D   The bold sentence says **"He went so far as to burn books of medical principles valued by the Doctors of Physick because he found them meaningless when applied to patients."** In other words Paracelsus destroyed medical "knowledge" that he deemed useless.

13.   The summary sentence is **"Paracelsus overcame obstacles to change both medical knowledge and the way medical knowledge was obtained,"** so we are looking for three ideas that will support this summary.

• "He made his medical theories accessible by teaching them to outsiders in contemporary languages"

• "He based his treatments on actual experience with patients rather than tradition or the dissection of dead bodies"

• "He lost his position as a university professor, but his theories gained acceptance after his death"

"He made his medical theories accessible by teaching them to outsiders in contemporary languages" should be used because it mentions a way Paracelsus changed the way medical knowledge was obtained. "He based his treatments on actual experience with patients rather than tradition or the dissection of dead bodies" should be used because it describes a way Paracelsus changed medical knowledge. "He worked with village apothecaries to make reliable treatments affordable to the common people" should not be used because it is not mentioned in the passage. "He perfected a method of using leeches to draw out blood from wounds" should not be used because it is not located in the passage. "He lost his position as a university professor, but his theories gained acceptance after his death" should be used because it describes one of the obstacles Paracelsus overcame to change medicine. "He revised the Hippocratic oath to include a promise not to harm patients" should not be used because it is not in the passage.

READING DRILL #13 ANSWERS

1. **D** Answer choice (D) contradicts the part of the passage that states that "His machine, called the Bessemer converter, made possible the mass production of steel. The differences between the new and old processes were enormous. The cost of producing steel fell ten-fold." Therefore (D) is the answer.

2. **D** The passage states that "steel found only limited application. Ships, bridges, railroad rails, and axles were still constructed with wrought iron, while steel was only used for smaller items, such as cutlery, tools, and springs" which indicates that steel was used only on small items. Therefore the answer is (D).

3. **D** This is a Vocabulary in Context question so use context clues to find the answer. The passage states that "whereas it had been made previously in blocks of 40 or 50 pounds each, three to five tons of iron could now be changed into steel in a matter of minutes." This sentence is closest in meaning to "produced quickly" so (D) is the answer.

4. **D** The passage states that steel had a "superior performance" so the answer is (D).

5. **D** The passage states that the Bessemer furnace was found while people "were working to find a less expensive method of making" steel. Therefore the answer is (D).

6. **A** The passage states that the Bessemer furnace "heated air at melted iron in a furnace burned out the impurities that made the iron brittle" therefore the answer is (A).

7. **B** This is a Vocabulary in Context question so use context clues to find the answer. The passage states that "Although several of them arrived independently at the same solution, it was Henry Bessemer who took credit." This indicates that different people individually came up with the furnace as a solution. Therefore (B) is the credited answer.

8. **C** The passage claims that during the Bessemer process "a blast of heated air at melted iron in a furnace burned out the impurities" so the answer is (C).

9. **B** The passage states that "prospectors discovered huge new deposits of iron ore in the mountains" so the answer is (B).

10. **B** The fourth paragraph argues that "Bessemer rails helped shape the industrial development of the nation, as manufacturers east of the Mississippi River became connected at all times to the growing markets in the West" so the answer is (B).

11. **B** The final sentence of the passage shows that "In 1870 only 77,000 tons of steel were produced in America, but by the turn of the century thirty years later, annual production had mushroomed to over eleven million tons." The word "mushroomed" here most closely means increased so the answer is (B).

12.   You should insert the sentence at the fourth insertion point.

          The added sentence adds an item to the list of things steel can produce which is primarily discussed in the fourth paragraph.

READING DRILL #14 ANSWERS

1. **C** The passage states that the letter "demonstrates the severity of the problem." The credited response is (C).

2. **D** This is a Vocabulary in Context question so use context clues to find the answer. The passage states that "before the agricultural development of the Midwest and West altered the natural balance of wildlife, there were frequent migrations of Rocky Mountain locusts." The word "altered" most closely means "changed" so the answer is (D).

3. **C** The passage indicates that the locust swarms were numerous in the text that states that "great hordes of these insects used to darken the skies on the plains east of the Rocky Mountains, often destroying crops. The following letter written by a Missouri farmer in 1875 graphically demonstrates the severity of the problem." Therefore the answer is (C).

4. **D** The highlighted sentence says "The seriousness of damage from the locusts in Nebraska is indicated by The Grasshopper Constitution, a revision of the original state constitution to include policies to reckon with the economic problems." In other words, the state of Nebraska had to modify its constitution to deal with the locust problem.

5. **D** The passage states that "a revision of the original state constitution to include policies to reckon with the economic problems" which means the state was attempting to "solve" the problem. The credited answer is (D).

6.　**Even so, there was a serious outbreak as late as 1938 in the Midwest of the United States and Canada.**

The question asks about the last outbreak. This sentence not only mentions the year of the outbreak but it also says "as late as" which is a clue that is a more recent outbreak.

7.　A　The passage states that "Locust swarms are large and can lay waste to everything in their path, but despite the difficulties humans have in combating them, they are not unstoppable." In other words locusts destroy everything. Therefore (A) is the answer.

8.　B　The passage states that "For locusts, the primary control mechanisms are weather and natural predators. For example, the Rocky Mountain locust is native to regions of high altitude and low rainfall. When a swarm of Rocky Mountain locusts migrates into a different climate in search of food, it can be wiped out with astonishing speed by a few weeks of extreme temperatures and rain." In other words it is surprising how fast a locust population can be eliminated an the answer is (B).

9.　B　The passage states that "When a swarm of Rocky Mountain locusts migrates into a different climate in search of food, it can be wiped out with astonishing speed by a few weeks of extreme temperatures and rain." Therefore the answer is (B).

10.　C　The passage states that "spiders, dragonflies, and hair worms are other invertebrates that prey on locusts" so the answer is (C).

11.　C　The passage claims that "locusts migrate into a different climate in search of food." Therefore the answer is (C).

12.　**These forms of locusts are apparently natural adaptations, designed to spread locust populations out when they become too crowded.**

This paragraph argues that "The migratory locust swarms that cause that sort of devastation arise under extreme environmental pressures, such as overcrowding and climate changes."

READING DRILL #15 ANSWERS

1.　D　The passage states that "Each kachina is said to possess not only a specific personality but also a lesson to **impart to** the members of the village. These personalities include chiefs who bring lessons of wisdom, women who teach motherly values." Therefore, **impart to** most clearly means teach or deliver and the answer is (D).

2.　C　The passage indicates that the various kachina "personalities include chiefs who bring lessons of wisdom, women who teach motherly values, and demons or ogres who **attend to** serious issues of discipline and behavior." Each personality is responsible for a different type of lesson. Therefore the answer is (C).

3. C   The topic sentence of the second paragraph states "Each kachina is said to possess not only a specific personality but also a lesson to **impart to** the members of the village." Therefore the answer is (C).

4. C   The passage states that "there are, however, also clown-like characters who bring **comic relief** to ceremonies that would otherwise be entirely solemn." The comic relief is to create a break in the seriousness of the ceremony so the answer is (C).

5. B   The bolded sentence is "**By breaking various taboos and transgressing boundaries set up by society, the Koshari Kachina provide examples to the younger members of the tribe of unacceptable conduct.**" In other words, these Kachina show children bad behavior that they should not do. Therefore the answer is (B).

6. A   The sentence with the highlighted word states that "each doll, traditionally made from the root of the cottonwood tree, is carved in the image of a particular kachina and is believed to have a small bit of the kachina residing within it." In this sentence it refers to the subject of the sentence which is the doll so the answer is (A).

7. A   The passage states that "The Koshari Kachina, for example, is usually portrayed holding a slice of watermelon, a symbol of the clown's gluttonous nature" as an example of these motifs. Therefore the answer is (A).

8.   **On the night of the winter solstice, dancers welcome the kachina back to human settlements by donning masks, each of which represents a particular spirit.**

        While the other sentences discuss some aspects, this sentence clearly links the wearing of the mask to the invitation of the kachina to the village.

9. B   The passage states that "They are incised with intricate symbols and often carry accessories, such as arrows or baskets, and are highly valued by collectors." As it is used intricate most nearly means detailed so the answer is (B).

10. B   The passage states that "Nowadays, the most common practice for many doll-makers is to use long-lasting acrylic paints, but some have begun to return to traditional mineral and plant pigments. The dolls are made with great care. They are incised with intricate symbols and often carry accessories, such as arrows or baskets, and are highly valued by collectors." Therefore you can eliminate (A), (C), and (D) and the credited answer is (B).

11. D   The passage states that historians disagree in the sentence that claims "Some historians say that the first dolls were given to women and children merely as representatives of the spirits, while others believe that they were aids in teaching children about the kachina." Therefore the answer is (D).

12. B   The passage never mentions the colors of paint that are used in the making of kachina dolls.

Part IV
Writing Review

Chapter 7
Writing Stategies

This section of the TOEFL measures your ability to communicate in an academic environment. This is supposed to check to see if you can write a college-level paper when you get to college. There are only two writing tasks, and they combine many of the qualities present in the Reading, Listening, and Speaking sections. On the Writing section, you'll be asked to do the following:

> * **Read** a passage on an academic subject, **listen** to a lecture on the same topic, and **write** an essay that discusses the relationship between the two. You'll have three minutes to read and 20 minutes to respond.
> * **Write** an essay that states, explains, and supports your position on an issue. You'll have 30 minutes to write this essay.
>
> You will have 50 minutes to complete both tasks.

WRITING SECTION DIRECTIONS

It is important to note that your first writing task will require both a reading and listening part, so you'll need to leave your headset on. Your essay must be typed, so you should have some familiarity with the keyboard before you take the TOEFL. The word processor used for the TOEFL is very simple; it only has *cut*, *copy*, and *paste* functions.

For the first task, you will have three minutes to read a passage. After that time is finished, the passage is removed from the screen, and you will listen to a lecture on the same topic. You may take notes during the reading and the lecture. When the lecture is finished, you'll have 20 minutes to write an essay on the relationship between the reading and the lecture. Your response must *not* include personal opinions. The reading passage will reappear on the screen for your reference.

The second task is much simpler. You will have 30 minutes to write a response to a prompt. There is no reading or lecture; you *are* asked to provide your personal views on a subject.

Because you will be reading, then listening, then writing, it is a good idea to take notes as you're going along to make sure you're getting the main ideas. Only do this, however, if you feel comfortable with note-taking.

HOW THE WRITING SECTION IS SCORED

Your TOEFL essays are graded on a 0 to 5 scale. A top-scoring essay on the TOEFL accomplishes the following:

- addresses the topic and the task
- is well organized and uses appropriate examples
- displays unity, progress, and coherence
- displays consistent facility in the use of language

It is worth noting that only one of the four criteria focuses on your use of language. The rest are concerned with how well you complete the task and how organized your writing is. So keep in mind that overall structure and content is more important than perfect grammar.

WRITING SECTION STRATEGIES

There are a few things to keep in mind when writing your essays for the TOEFL. As with the Speaking section, the graders are not expecting perfection. They realize that you are essentially writing the first draft of an essay. Given the limited amount of time provided, they expect you to make a few grammatical mistakes and misspell a few words. Furthermore, in many ways the graders are looking more at *how* you write, not *what* you write. The structure and organization of your essay is just as important as the content of your essay.

When writing your essay, be aware of the following important points:

- Make sure you answer the question appropriately.
- Make sure your essay is long enough.
- Make sure your essay is clearly organized.

Paying attention to these three basic points will put you on the right track. Let's look at them in further detail.

Basic Principle #1: Make Sure You Answer the Question Appropriately

One of the first things the graders will look at when reading your essay is if you answered the question in the prompt. Well-written essays that don't address the task will lose points. Therefore, it is important that you know about the two different tasks you will be asked to do.

The first task asks you to **summarize** and **relate** the points in a lecture to those in a reading. Thus, your essay should contain *only* facts from the material. All you are expected to do is report the main points mentioned and show how they are related to each other. You should *not* give your opinion on any of the topics. The first task should be written entirely in the third person—that is, using words such as *he, she, the professor, the student,* and so on. You should never use *I* or *me* in the first essay.

The second task requires you to state your **opinion.** This task requires you to argue what option or choice you believe to be better. Thus, the essay should be written in the first person—it's acceptable to use *I* and *my* for the second essay.

It is important that you understand the tasks. Knowing exactly what your purpose is makes the essays easier to write.

Basic Principle #2: Make Sure Your Essay Is Long Enough

On the TOEFL, quantity makes a difference. To a grader, a longer essay is a better essay. Why? Because a longer essay shows the grader that you are comfortable writing and are able to produce a sustained, focused piece. When writing, you must make sure your essay falls within the TOEFL's suggested guidelines for length.

- For the first task, the TOEFL states that an effective response is between 150 to 225 words.
- A minimum of 300 words is required for the second task.

Although these word counts may seem intimidating, they're not as bad as you may think. For example, the section that you are now reading is more than 100 words. In fact, a 200-word essay basically consists of an introduction, one or two body paragraphs, and a conclusion—about the same length as half of this page. That's it.

A 300-word essay is approximately two-thirds of this page. You'll find that when you use the essay templates in this chapter, you shouldn't have any problem writing 300 words, but you should nonetheless count the words of your practice essays to make sure they are long enough.

Basic Principle #3: Make Sure Your Essay Is Clearly Organized

Organized essays are easy to read. Essays that are easy to read are easy to understand. TOEFL graders like both of those qualities. Your written responses on the TOEFL should contain the following:

- **An introduction,** containing your thesis statement
- **Body paragraphs,** containing examples and details that support your thesis
- **A conclusion,** containing a final restatement of your thesis
- **Appropriate transitions,** linking your paragraphs and ideas together

Now would be a good time to return to Core Concept: Writing, especially if you haven't read through it yet. That section provides all the necessary information on how to organize your essay and use transitions.

BASIC APPROACH

You will achieve a good score on the TOEFL Writing section if you do the following:

1. **Know what you're going to write before you write.** Master the writing templates in this chapter so you are confident on test day.
2. **Organize your essay first.** Don't just start writing; spend a few minutes outlining your essay. It will make writing it much easier.
3. **Consider your audience.** TOEFL graders are trained to look for certain things in an essay. Make sure your essay contains these key elements.
4. **Use your time wisely.** You have only 20 or 30 minutes to write. Make efficient use of your time.

Let's look at each of these steps.

Step 1: Know What You're Going to Write

The biggest danger in trying to write under timed conditions is writer's block—that is, you have absolutely no idea what to write. While you struggle with how to put your thoughts on paper, valuable time slips away. Fortunately, there is an easy solution to this problem: Know exactly what you need to write *before* you sit down at the testing center.

We're going to look at templates for each of the writing tasks. Use these templates and familiarize yourself with their basic structures. That way, all you'll have to do is adjust the template to the specific topic.

Template #1: Casting Doubt on a Lecture

For the first essay, you will usually be asked to perform the following task:

> Summarize the points made in the lecture, explaining how they cast doubt on the reading.

Essay Tip: There are only a few commonly used essay questions on the first TOEFL Writing section. Use our tips on the following pages, and you can walk into the test totally prepared.

The template for this task is as follows:

Paragraph #1: Introduction

I. Topic sentence
In the lecture, the (professor/teacher/instructor) **made several points about** (topic).

II. State main idea of lecture
The (professor/teacher/instructor) **argues that** (the main idea of the lecture).

III. Transition/main idea of reading
However, the reading contends that (the main idea of the reading).

IV. Thesis statement
The professor's lecture casts doubt on the reading by using a number of points that are contrary to (the main idea of the reading).

Paragraph #2: Body Paragraph

I. Transition/point #1 from lecture
The first point that the (professor/teacher/instructor) **uses to cast doubt on the reading is** (point #1 from lecture).

II. Detail for point #1
According to the (professor/teacher/instructor), (detail for point #1 from the lecture).

III. Opposing point from reading
(Point #1) **differs from the reading in that the reading states** (point #1 of the reading).

IV. Explanation of relationship between reading and lecture
The point made by the (professor/lecturer/instructor) **casts doubt on the reading because** (how lecture is different from reading).

Paragraph #3: Body Paragraph

I. Transition/point #2 from lecture
Another point that the (professor/teacher/instructor) **uses to cast doubt on the reading is** (point #2 from lecture).

II. Detail for point #2
The (professor/teacher/instructor) **claims that** (detail for point #2 from the lecture).

III. Opposing point from reading
However, the reading states (point #2 from reading).

IV. Explanation of relationship between reading and lecture
This point is contradicted by (point #2 from lecture).

Paragraph #4: Conclusion

I. Topic sentence
In conclusion, the points made in the lecture contrast with the reading.

II. Summary
(Points #1 and #2 from the lecture) **demonstrate that** (main idea of the reading) **is in doubt.**

The words in bold are suggestions; you don't have to use them exactly. You may also find that you have time to write a third body paragraph. If so, repeat the formula from the first two body paragraphs. However, your writing should still follow the general pattern established in the outline.

Template #2: Showing Support for a Reading Passage

You may also see a prompt like the following:

Summarize the points made in the lecture, explaining how they support the reading.

This task is simply the opposite of the first. Thus the template is fairly similar.

Paragraph #1: Introduction
I. Topic sentence
In the lecture, the (professor/teacher/instructor) **made several points about** (the topic).
II. State main idea of lecture
The (professor/teacher/instructor) **argues that** (main idea of the lecture).
III. Transition/main idea of reading
The points made by the (professor/teacher/instructor) **agree with** (main idea of the reading passage).
IV. Thesis statement
In fact, the examples used by the (professor/teacher/instructor) **support** (main idea of the reading passage).

Paragraph #2: Body Paragraph
I. Transition/point #1 from lecture
The first point that the (professor/teacher/instructor) **uses to support the reading is** (point #1 from the lecture).
II. Detail for point #1
According to the (professor/teacher/instructor), (detail for point #1 from the lecture).
III. Opposing point from reading
(Point #1) **supports the reading, which holds that** (point #1 from the reading passage).
IV. Explanation of relationship between reading and lecture
The point made by the (professor/lecturer/instructor) **supports the reading because** (why lecture agrees with the reading).

Paragraph #3: Body Paragraph

I. Transition/point #2 from lecture
Furthermore, the (professor/teacher/instructor) **bolsters the reading by stating that** (point #2 from the lecture).

II. Detail for point #2
The (professor/teacher/instructor) **claims that** (detail for point #2 from the lecture).

III. Opposing point from reading
This point agrees with the reading, which contends that (point #2 from the reading).

IV. Explanation of relationship between reading and lecture
The (point #2 from lecture) **shows the truth of the reading because** (how point #2 agrees with the reading).

Paragraph #4: Conclusion

I. Topic sentence
In conclusion, the points made in the lecture support the reading.

II. Summary
(Points #1 and #2 from the lecture) **demonstrate that** (main idea of the reading) **is valid.**

Template #3: Using Specific Details and Examples to Support Your Opinion

The second task on the TOEFL simply asks for your opinion on a matter. The prompt will look something like the example shown below.

Do you agree or disagree with the following statement?

(statement)

Use specific details and examples to support your answer.

For the second task, we'll use the following template:

Paragraph #1: Introduction

I. Topic sentence/paraphrase prompt
The issue at hand is (choice offered by the prompt).

II. Interpret the prompt
This issue is (important/difficult/troubling) **because** (what is important/difficult/troubling about the prompt).

III. State your thesis
I believe that (state your choice) **is the better option because** (reasons why you believe your option is preferable).

Paragraph #2: Body Paragraph
  I. Transition/first reason
  (Your choice of options) **is preferable because** (reason #1).
  II. Detail for reason #1
  (Details about reason #1)
  III. Tie reason #1 back to thesis
  Because (details about reason #1), **I think that** (your choice) **is superior to** (the other option).

Paragraph #3: Body Paragraph
  I. Transition/second reason
  Additionally, (your choice) **is better because** (reason #2).
  II. Detail for reason #2
  (Details about reason #2)
  III. Tie reason #2 back to thesis
  Based on (details about reason #2), (your choice) **is a better option than** (the other option).

Paragraph #4: Body Paragraph
  I. Transition/third reason
  Finally, I think (your choice) **is the right choice because** (reason #3).
  II. Detail for reason #3
  (Details about reason #3).
  III. Tie reason #3 back to thesis
  I like (your choice) **over** (the other option) **due to** (details about reason #3).

Paragraph #5: Conclusion
  I. Transition/restate thesis
  Ultimately, I feel that (your choice) **is the correct one.**
  II. Final statement
  I believe this because (why you believe your choice is best).

In summary, familiarize yourself with these templates. If you know exactly what your essay is supposed to look like, you'll have a much easier time writing.

Step 2: Organize Your Essay

In the first step, we looked at how your essay should *be structured*. Now we need to talk about what your essay will *contain*. Before you start writing, spend about five minutes brainstorming examples and points for your essay. Failing to do so may lead you to write an essay that lacks focus and coherence.

For the first task, you'll be presented with a short reading passage. While reading, take notes on the main idea and some of the major facts presented. Your notes do not have to be very detailed—you'll be able to refer back to the passage while you are writing. However, it is important to know the general idea of the reading so that you can relate it back to the lecture.

During the lecture, try to note the major points presented by the professor. There will usually be three to five points, but you won't need all of them: two or three points will be sufficient for the task. You will not be able to hear the lecture again, so it is important to remember some of the points.

Try to organize your notes in the following way:

Reading:

Main idea: _____

Example/reason: _____

Example/reason: _____

Example/reason: _____

Remember, if it's too difficult to read and take notes, then do not attempt to do so. The reading passage will be available for reference while you write. For the lecture, the main idea is generally opposite that of the reading, so don't worry about noting that. The examples offered in the lecture are the parts you have to concentrate on. During the lecture, try to organize your notes as follows.

Lecture:

Point #1: _____

Detail #1: _____

Point #2: _____

Detail #2: _____

Point #3: _____

Detail #3: _____

Even if you are unable to write down the details for the example, you'll need to try to remember them so you can refer to them in your essay. If you don't mention specific points from the lecture, you will receive a lower score.

For the second task, it is very important that you come up with good reasons for your viewpoint. You need to tell the reader why you believe your opinion is better. Here's a good way to organize your thoughts.

Issue:

Your opinion: _____

Why? _____

Reason #1: _____

Detail #1: _____

Reason #2: _____

Detail #2: _____

Reason #3: _____

Detail #3: _____

Step 3: Consider Your Audience

TOEFL graders are trained to look for certain features in your writing. By ensuring that your essay contains these features, you'll improve your score. Similarly, there are some elements to avoid in your writing. Make sure your essay contains the following:

1. **An introduction, body paragraphs, and a conclusion.**
2. **Specific examples.** Your essay must use specific examples. The more detail you use, the better your essay will be.
3. **Transitions.** One of the things TOEFL graders look for in an essay is "unity and coherence." That means that all the ideas must flow easily. They should be linked together with appropriate transitions.

In addition, you'll want to avoid the following:

1. **Repeating phrases from the reading or prompt word for word.** Always put the examples and reasons into your own words. Although repeating a word or two is acceptable, you should *never* copy long phrases directly from the text on screen. TOEFL graders will penalize you for this.
2. **Writing your essay as one long paragraph.** Make sure you divide your essay into separate paragraphs. *Do not* just write a single block of text.
3. **Including material not relevant to the task.** Your essay must remain on topic. *Do not* include any reasons or examples that do not connect or relate to the task.

By keeping these points in mind, you'll ensure that your essay is well received by the TOEFL graders.

Step 4: Use Your Time Wisely

If you had unlimited time, you would surely be able to achieve a top score on the Writing section. Unfortunately, your time on the TOEFL is extremely limited. Thus, you must make sure to use your time wisely. The following tables provide a good guide for how to spend your time.

Task #1: 20 minutes

Time	Task
5 minutes	Organize your essay.
2 minutes	Write your introduction.
10 minutes	Write your body paragraphs.
2 minutes	Write your conclusion.
1 minute	Proofread your essay to correct any mistakes.

Task #2: 30 minutes

Time	Task
7 minutes	Organize your essay.
2 minutes	Write your introduction.
16 minutes	Write your body paragraphs.
2 minutes	Write your conclusion.
3 minutes	Proofread your essay to correct any mistakes.

To stick to these guidelines, you'll have to know exactly what your essay is going to look like. Use the templates from Step 1 to focus as you read.

Now you're ready to try some practice writing drills.

The next chapter contains writing drills for the Reading, Listening, and Writing question type. We have provided sample high- and low-scoring essays as guidances; however we also recommend that you check in with a English-speaking teacher for more guidance and feedback.

Chapter 8
Writing Drills

Now you're ready to practice the Writing section. We've provided lined pages on which to write your responses, but it would be better to practice typing your answers on a computer because that's how you'll be doing it on the actual TOEFL. Try the following practice prompts. Remember to register your book online so that you can access the audio tracks. After you've finished, read through the sample essays at the end of the chapter to get an idea of what TOEFL graders are looking for in the essay responses.

WRITING DRILL #1

Read the following passage about "the tragedy of the commons."

The "tragedy of the commons" is a concept invented by biologist Garrett Hardin in the 1960s. It describes how resources are depleted when people overuse them without penalty. Hardin used the example of land shared among several farmers. He argued that a fixed piece of land produces a fixed amount of grass, meaning that there is a limit to the number of animals it can feed. But Hardin said that each farmer has an incentive to feed more animals than the pastureland can support. The reasoning was this: A farmer kept all the wealth gained by adding an extra animal (its value) but only suffered a fraction of the loss from using the pasture beyond its limits (loss of pasture quality). The rest of the loss was shared with other farmers. Therefore, giving all users free access to resources encourages each to take more than he needs, because he receives all the advantages but only part of the disadvantages.

Some environmentalists have applied Hardin's idea to fishing spots in key rivers, lakes, and areas of the ocean. They point out that many species of fish that were once numerous have become depopulated through overfishing. Some species have been close to disappearing. These environmentalists call for more government involvement in fishing. Since the government is responsible to all fishing companies equally, it is in a position to set fair regulations on the number of fish that may be legally caught in a given season. Government regulation is the best way to ensure that overfishing stops and fish populations are restored.

 Now play Track #1 and listen to part of a lecture on the topic you just read about.

Once you've finished listening to the lecture, summarize the points made in the lecture you just heard, explaining how they cast doubt on the contents of the reading. You may refer to the passage as you write.

_____

_____

_____

_____

_____

_____

_____

_____

_____

_____

WRITING DRILL #2

Read the following passage about whether or not the Egyptians ever sailed to the Americas.

The question of whether the ancient Egyptians discovered the Americas centuries before Columbus remains unanswered. The conditions that would have made such a voyage possible are, however, relatively obvious. In 1969, the scholar Thor Heyerdahl used boats built according to ancient Egyptian design to test the likelihood of a successful crossing of the Atlantic Ocean. The boat was fashioned from papyrus reeds, as such a craft would have been in the second century BC.

Heyerdahl and his team had to address three main questions in making their journey. One question was whether the Egyptians, starting from Africa, might have been able to reach the fast-moving currents that would draw their small boat westward toward the Americas. The researchers, using their knowledge of the currents and winds, were able to reach favorable currents with little difficulty.

It was also questionable whether enough food and water could be stowed aboard such a boat to last the duration of so long a voyage on sea. By carefully selecting their provisions, the researchers were able to carry along enough to last them through the passage over the Atlantic.

Yet a third question was whether a boat made of reeds could withstand the voyage without being worn away by constant exposure to sun and seawater. One of Heyerdahl's boats successfully navigated from Morocco, on the northwest coast of Africa, to a point off the shore of Barbados, an island in the Caribbean Sea and near the South American continent.

 Now play Track #2 and listen to part of a lecture on the topic you just read about.

Once you've finished listening to the lecture, summarize the points made in the lecture you just heard, explaining how they cast doubt on the contents of the reading. You may refer to the passage as you write.

_____
_____
_____
_____
_____
_____
_____
_____
_____
_____
_____
_____
_____
_____
_____

WRITING DRILL #3

Read the following passage about different methods of preserving food.

Preserving food for long periods requires inhibiting the growth of microorganisms that cause it to decay, such as molds and mildew. This involves making conditions inhospitable to bacteria, as in refrigeration, dehydration, or sealing in airtight containers. Sterilizing the food before storage, through heat or irradiation, is often beneficial.

Flash-freezing was invented by the American Clarence Birdseye in the 1920s. It would have been impossible before then because it requires high pressure and an extremely efficient, fast-acting freezing unit. If food is plunged from room temperature to freezing very quickly, its texture and flavor are not ruined. The technique was first used on fish, but is most famous as a way of making vegetables to consumers through the winter.

The process of freeze-drying uses both freezing and the removal of water to convert food into a state in which it can be held for long periods. The first freeze-dried food was coffee, produced by the French company Nestle. Nestle's management had been asked by Brazil for ideas about what to do with that country's coffee surplus. Freeze-drying produced a powdered coffee that could be easily reconstituted into the familiar drink with the addition of hot water.

Freeze-drying consists essentially of two stages that, like simple flash-freezing, can only be achieved through machines. First, a super-cold refrigeration unit is used to bring the food far below the freezing temperature of water. Next, a vacuum pump is applied. The extreme low pressure it creates allows the water to sublimate, that is, to turn from solid ice to vapor instantly. The water vapor can then be drawn away, leaving dried food ready for long-term storage.

 Now play Track #3 and listen to part of a lecture on the topic you just read about.

Once you've finished listening to the lecture, summarize the points made in the lecture you just heard, explaining how they cast doubt on the contents of the reading. You may refer to the passage as you write.

_____

_____

_____

_____

_____

_____

_____

_____

_____

_____

_____

_____

WRITING DRILL #4

Read the following passage about the similarities between different ancient civilizations.

There are so many similarities between certain ancient civilizations that some researchers have concluded that knowledge must have been communicated between them, despite their distance in time or space.

One such pair is the ancient Egyptians and the Maya, a civilization that flowered in what is now Mexico in the 1400s. Both peoples had a very sophisticated grasp of astronomy, to the point that the complexity and accuracy of their calendar systems astonishes modern scholars. The similarities don't end there, though. For example, both the Egyptians and the Maya developed a calendar of 360 days, using a formula to add the extra 5 days to complete the solar year.

Possibly the most striking similarity between the civilizations, however, is their use of pyramids. Both cultures used their pyramids for important ritual purposes. The surfaces of their pyramids look similar, because both were built from pieces of stone laid side-by-side like bricks. They also positioned their pyramids very prominently, though they would have towered over other buildings in either civilization no matter where they were built.

There are more detailed physical resemblances that indicate that the same pyramid style must have been passed through history from Egypt to the Maya. In both societies, pyramids tended to be built with square bases, with their sides oriented exactly north, south, east, and west. From the base, layers of stone rose in a stair-step pattern. The entryways were small doors near ground level, with a network of tunnels inside the structure.

 Now play Track #4 and listen to part of a lecture on the topic you just read about.

Once you've finished listening to the lecture, summarize the points made in the lecture you just heard, explaining how they cast doubt on the contents of the reading. You may refer to the passage as you write.

_____
_____
_____
_____
_____
_____
_____
_____
_____
_____
_____
_____
_____
_____
_____

Chapter 9
Writing Drills:
Answers and
Explanations

Read through the following sample responses to the drills you completed in the previous chapter, and compare your essays with them. If possible, have a friend who is a native speaker or highly proficient in English look over your essays. As always, your writing does not have to match ours exactly. Just check to see if your essay accomplishes the important points highlighted in the high-scoring essays.

WRITING DRILL #1 ANSWER

Below is the audio transcript of the lecture:

Narrator: Now listen to part of a lecture on the topic you just read about:

Professor: Okay, if you've all done the reading, you understand what the tragedy of the commons is and how it can cause problems in the use of natural resources, particularly fishing. But the positive role of government regulation isn't as clear cut as it may seem. The government may not have a single favorite fishing company, but sometimes it favors *all* the fishing companies over the fish! When fishing companies complain that lower fish populations are causing them financial problems, some governments actually give grant money to fishing companies or raise limits on the size of catches in order to help them. That encourages companies to keep overfishing.

And then there's the problem of, if the government controls everything, it has the job of policing all the bodies of water—an almost impossible job. What some countries have found effective is giving fishing rights to individuals, or individual companies. What happens is, you get the right to all the fish in, say, a certain section of a lake. Other people have rights to the neighboring sections. Now, the fishing right has value. You paid for it, like a piece of land or a house. And you may want to sell it later, or leave it to your children—again like a house—so you'll need to make sure you leave plenty of fish, or your fishing rights will be worthless. Also, you'll guard your area against people who would steal the fish...well, for the same reason. And you'll just have your area to concentrate on, so you can manage. Your goal is to keep the value of your investment, but the effect is that you end up protecting the fish populations in the process.

Narrator: Summarize the points made in the lecture you just heard, explaining how they cast doubt on the contents of the reading. You may refer to the passage as you write.

Now let's look at a couple of sample essays.

High-Scoring Example

In the lecture, the professor made several points about regulations of fishing spots. The professor stated that government regulations may not solve the overfishing problem that is caused by the tragedy of the commons. The lecture is different from the reading because according to the reading government regulations would likely solve the overfishing problem. The professor offers another solution by saying that offering individual fishing rights would end overfishing in certain areas.

The first point in the lecture is that governments sometimes prefer fishing companies to the fish. When fishermen complain about low fish levels the government may allow them to fish more which makes the problem worse. Another negative thing about government regulations is that governments cannot police regulations of all water. The reading is different because it states that governments could solve overfishing by limiting the amount of fish that companies can catch.

The second point in the lecture is that giving fishing rights to individuals could solve the problem of overfishing better than government regulation. The professor says that by giving people rights to fish in certain areas, there would be less overfishing because people would protect the value of the fishing rights by maintaining the fish population. The professor also says individuals would also have a reason to police their part of the water.

In conclusion, the professor challenges the claim in the reading that government regulations could solve the overfishing problem caused by the tragedy of the commons and provides another solution to the problem.

Score: 5 This response received a score of 5. It has all the important elements required by the prompt.

- The essay is well-organized and stays on topic throughout.
- There are two examples discussed in the lecture and both are mentioned with details in the response.
- The conclusion appropriately sums up the passage.

Lower-Scoring Example

There are a few different ways to solve the problem of overfishing in lakes. Fisherman sometimes fish too much and make the population of fish lower so that other people cannot fish in those lakes.

One way to solve the problem of overfishing is through government regulation.

Governments can put limits on the number of fish a company catches. This may not always work because governments cannot always get police on lakes.

Another way to solve the problem is by selling rights to fish in certain places. People who own rights could protect their fish and sell the rights whenever they want.

Score: 2 This essay received a score of a 2. Here's why:

- It does address a couple of points from the lecture and is organized into a paragraphs.
- However, it does not mention the connection between the reading and the lecture.
- The essay is too short.

The writer needs to better organize this essay and develop examples that detail the connection between the reading and the lecture.

WRITING DRILL #2 ANSWER

Below is the audio transcript of the lecture:

Narrator: Now listen to part of a lecture on the topic you just read about:

Professor: Okay, if we're going to talk about the possibility that the ancient Egyptians sailed from Egypt to the Americas about 3,500 years ago, let's bear some things in mind. One is that the first people to make the voyage would be missing a lot of the information we have available today. We know, from centuries of experience, where the winds and currents are that will help carry a ship from Africa to the Caribbean Sea. The first Egyptians to make such a voyage wouldn't even have known that two continents and the islands of the Caribbean were waiting for them on the opposite side of the Atlantic. Given all the guesswork involved, the likelihood that they would have had the luck to run into the most favorable winds and currents, and that they would have kept going farther and farther from home without knowing there was anything up ahead, is not very high.

Uh, and then you have to think about the boat itself. There's no evidence that the Egyptians ever sailed far from the coast. The boats always came back to shore for the night, so it's difficult to assume that sailors would have packed enough food and water to last more than one day. That's why there wasn't much storage space designed into their boats, though the boats were *capable* of holding more than you might expect. Also, the papyrus reeds from which their boats were made were not very sturdy. Morocco, from which some reed boats sailed in the 1960s in an attempt to show…that the Egyptians could have gone from Africa to the Americas, is actually a few thousand miles closer to the Americas than Egypt. And those boats broke apart before they'd actually come to shore in the Americas. That is, they weren't even really able to make it all the way across from Morocco.

Narrator: Summarize the points made in the lecture you just heard, explaining how they cast doubt on the contents of the reading.

Now let's look at a couple of sample essays.

High-Scoring Example

The reading states that it may have been possible for ancient Egyptians to travel to the Americas on boats. The lecture provides three reasons to doubt the conclusion of the reading and says that it is unlikely that Egyptians discovered the Americas.

The lecture agrees that it may have been possible for the Egyptians to find the fast curents. However, the first reason the lecture says it is unlikely that Egyptians discovered the Americas is that they did not know the location of the fast currents or even know that there was land that far from their homes. The professor said that the Egyptians probably would not have kept going that far without knowing there was land somewhere.

Secondly, the lecture states that even if the Egyptian boats had space for enough food and water to last the journey, the Egyptian sailors never sailed for more than a day. The professor says that since they did not usually sail for long journeys it is unlikely that they took many provisions. This is different from the reading that says Egyptians could have fit enough food and water for a journey to the Americas.

The last reason the professor says that Egyptians probably did not discover the Americas was that there boats were not strong enough to make it all the way from Egypt to the Americas. The reading says that a reed boat could have made it from Morroco to Barbados. However, the lecture states that Egypt was farther away and that the reed boats barely made it as far as they did.

In conclusion, the professor challenges the claim in the reading that Egyptians may have discovered the Americas by offering three things that cast doubt on the possibilities in the reading.

Score: 5 This essay received a score of 5. It has all the important elements required by the prompt.

- The essay successfully selects the important points from the lecture and explains how they relate to the reading.
- The essay is well-organized and uses appropriate examples throughout.
- Minor spelling and grammar mistakes do not detract from the overall point.

Lower-Scoring Example

The professor answers the open questions mentioned in the passage about the possibility of the Egyptians discovering the Americas.

The first question is whether Egyptians would have found the routes to the Americas. The lecture says that it might have been possible but it was unlikely because the Egyptians did not know there was a place in the Americas.

The next question is whether Egyptians would have enough space to store food. The professor says that they could have stored enough food but they probably would not have taken that much food or water on the boats because they did not plan to be gone for more than a day.

The last question the professor answers is whether the boat was strong enough to make it that far. The professor says that a reed boat may have made it from Morrocco to Barbados but that it would not have made it from Egypt to the Americas.

Score: 3 This essay receives a score of 3 which is an average score on the TOEFL. There are some good things in this essay:

- The essay is well organized and contains several important points from the lecture.
- The essay uses detailed examples.

However, there are a few issues that prevent the essay from getting a higher score.

- The essay is too short and does not have a conclusion.
- The overall point of the essay fails to communicate the complete relationship between the lecture and the reading.

WRITING DRILL #3 ANSWER

Below is the audio transcript of the lecture:

Narrator: Now listen to part of a lecture on the topic you just read about:

Professor: There's something interesting about your reading for this week. As you'll remember, it described the invention of two methods of food preservation: flash-freezing and freeze-drying.

What's the interesting thing? The author seems to think that neither of these methods existed before the machine age, but he should have done more research. Both were techniques used by Native Americans for hundreds of years. In fact, Clarence Birdseye got the idea for flash-freezing from working with Inuit peoples. These Inuits lived in northern Canada, where there's super-cold icy water available. Birdseye noticed that when they preserved catches of fish by plunging the fish into this super-cold ice water so that they froze almost immediately, the fish still tasted fresh, even when cooked months later. The natural ice water performed the same function as mechanical freezers later did in his successful company.

Freeze-drying was used by the Incas of South America. The cold environment they used wasn't the North Pole, obviously, it was the very high Andes Mountains. High in the mountains, the temperature was very cold, especially at night. And the sunlight was very strong during the day, because the peaks are closer to the sun than lower areas, right? Also, the air is thin—well, it is up in the mountains. So the Incas learned that they could spread out potatoes—they did this with potatoes—at night. Overnight, the potatoes froze, and during the day, the low air pressure and strong sun caused the frozen water to evaporate very rapidly. So you had freeze-dried potatoes that were very light to carry and could be restored with water...just as if it'd been done in a machine. And this was hundreds of years ago.

Narrator: Summarize the points made in the lecture you just heard, explaining how they cast doubt on the contents of the reading.

Now let's look at a couple of sample essays.

High-Scoring Example

In the lecture, the professors talk about two groups of Native Americans that preserved food in ways the reading says is only possible with machines. The professors challenge the reading by saying that these people were using methods hundreds of years before machines.

The first group of Native Americans the lecture discusses is the Inuits. The professors say that the Inuits use a technique like flash freezing to preserve fish. They would dip the fish in really cold water and then store it for long periods. The reading says that flash freezing was discovered by a man named Birdseye and that it was possible only with machines. However, the Inuits were doing it without machines before Birdseye.

The other group of Native Americans the professor talks about are the Incas. They used a technique like freeze-drying to preserve potatoes in the mountains. The potatoes would have frozen overnight and then the sun would evaporate the water and made the potatoes light enough to store. The professor says that the reading is wrong because the Incas freeze dried potatoes hundreds of years before machines allowed the Nestle people to freeze dry coffee.

In conclusion, the lecture casts doubt on the claim in the reading that flash freezing and freeze drying methods were invented in the 20th century and were only possible by using machines. The professor challenges this claim by offering two examples of native peoples that used the methods for many years before machines.

Score: 5 This essay received a score of 5. It has all the important elements required by the prompt.

- The essay successfully selects the important points from the lecture and explains how they relate to the reading.
- The essay is well-organized and uses appropriate examples throughout.
- Minor spelling and grammar mistakes do not detract from the overall point.

Lower-Scoring Example

The reading says that flash freezing and freeze drying are done by machines but the professor says that Native Americans did not need machines to do it. They could flash freeze fish or freeze dry potatoes without machines. The Native American examples show how the reading is wrong and the professor is correct.

Score: 1 This essay received a score of only a 1, the lowest score possible. Here are some reasons why:

- Although the essay does address the topic, there is no organization. The essay contains only one paragraph.
- The examples lack sufficient details.
- The essay is too short.

WRITING DRILL #4 ANSWER

Below is the audio transcript of the lecture:

Narrator: Now listen to part of a lecture on the topic you just read about:

Professor: Sometimes, things that look similar or related on the surface turn out to be unrelated when you look more closely. Since we're talking about ancient cultures, I'd like to show you what I mean with a few examples.

Take the 360-day calendar. The actual number of days in a solar year is closer to 365, but 360 is an easier number to calculate mathematically, so many civilizations arrived at the 360-day calendar and then developed more accurate calendars later. That means you can't just look at two different civilizations and say, "Gee, they both used a 360-day calendar; they must have been in contact with each other somehow." The same with buildings built on a square base; most cultures learned about the square as they developed independently.

Even things that seem unique can be deceptive. The Egyptian and Mayan pyramids, for example, look similar. But their uses were different: The Egyptians used their pyramids as tombs to bury important people. The pyramids were put outside their cities, the way our cemeteries often are, and they were designed to be hard to enter. The Egyptians hid the entrances to their pyramids and sealed them when they were finished. Not the Maya—they built their pyramids right in the middle of the city, because they were used in religious ceremonies. The stair-step pattern of the sides? It was literally used for people to climb up to the top or to get to the entrance.

And the Egyptians used stones that they cut from quarries, very carefully shaped and polished with tools. The Maya picked up stones from the ground and used them without polishing; they used plaster to smooth the surface of their pyramids, and unlike the Egyptians, they sometimes painted designs on them. Not the same at all.

Narrator: Summarize the points made in the lecture you just heard, explaining how they cast doubt on the contents of the reading.

Now let's look at a couple of sample essays.

High-Scoring Example

In the lecture, the professor discusses several differences between two ancient civilizations. The reading states that the similarities between the Egyptians and Mayans is evidence that they must have communicated. However, the lecture says that the similarities do not mean they communicated. The professor gives two reasons that challenge the idea that the two groups communicated.

The first reason the professor gives for saying the Egyptians and Mayans probably did not communicate is that some things they came up with are the simplest solutions to a problem so they could have come up with them on their own. The reading says that the square building bases and the 360 day calendar prove the two cultures communicated but the professor says that they probably came up with these ideas independently without communicating.

The second thing the professor discussed were the many differences between Egyptian and Mayan pyramids. While the reading says that the pyramid similarities show the two groups must have communicated, the professor argues that the differences between pyramids show that the two did not communicate. The Egyptians used pyramids for tombs and the Mayans used pyramids for ceremones. The Egyptians made pyramids out of polished stone and sealed the entrances but the Mayans found stones to build their pyramids and built stairs to make it easy to use the pyramid.

In conclusion, the lecture says that Egyptians and Mayans did not communicate because similarities in discoveries of the two civilizations were just coincidental.

Score: 5 This essay received a score of 5. It has all the important elements required by the prompt.

- The essay successfully selects the important points from the lecture and explains how they relate to the reading.
- The essay is well-organized and uses appropriate examples throughout.
- Minor spelling and grammar mistakes do not detract from the overall point.

Lower-Scoring Example

The Egyptians and Mayans built pyramids that were similar but also somewhat different because they communicated with each other over a long distance.

The Egyptians and Mayans both built pyramids in important places in town and use square bases to build them. These similarities show that they probably communicated with each other.

The Mayans used pyramids for ceremonies and the Egyptians used pyramids for tombs though so they may not have communicated.

The similarities of the two groups makes it seem like they talked to each other but the differences say they may not have.

Score: 2 This essay received a score of a 2. Here's why:

- It does address a couple of points from the lecture and is organized into a paragraphs.
- However, it does not mention the connection between the reading and the lecture.
- The essay is too short.

The writer needs to better organize this essay and develop examples that detail the connection between the reading and the lecture.

NOTES

NOTES

NOTES

NOTES

NOTES

NOTES

NOTES

NOTES

NOTES

NOTES